TypeScript Blueprints

Build exciting end-to-end applications with TypeScript

Ivo Gabe de Wolff

BIRMINGHAM - MUMBAI

TypeScript Blueprints

First published: July 2016

Production reference: 1250716

Published by Packt Publishing Ltd.
Livery Place
35 Livery Street
Birmingham
B3 2PB, UK.
ISBN 978-1-78588-701-7

www.packtpub.com

Credits

Authors

Ivo Gabe de Wolff

Copy Editor

Safis Editing

Reviewer

Matthew Hill

Project Coordinator

Ulhas Kambali

Commissioning Editor

Kunal Parikh

Proofreader

Safis Editing

Acquisition Editor

Divya Poojari

Indexer

Rekha Nair

Content Development Editor

Prashanth G

Graphics

Jason Monteiro

Technical Editor

Shivani K. Mistry

Production Coordinator

Aparna Bhagat

About the Author

Ivo Gabe de Wolff has been a freelance developer under the name of ivogabe since 2012 and he is studying mathematics and computing sciences at Utrecht University. When he was eleven he started programming in Game Maker. Currently, he uses TypeScript on a daily basis. Recently, he has used TypeScript in lots of different environments, including mobile apps, servers, and command-line tools. Now he mainly specializes in NodeJS programming.

Furthermore, he is the author of various open source projects, including gulp-typescript. You can find his projects on *github.com/ivogabe*. If you want to read more about TypeScript, JavaScript, gulp, or Functional Programming, you can take a look at his blog at *dev.ivogabe.com*.

It required a lot of work to compose this book. I could not have done this without the help of these people:

The team at Packt Publishing and the reviewers of this book, because of their precise feedback and hard work. This has helped me a lot to improve the quality of this book.

My fellow students, for brainstorming and helping on specific topics.

My teachers at Utrecht University, for giving inspiration and challenging me on various topics. I especially want to thank Jurriaan Hage for supervising my thesis.

Finally, my family, for their support and tips, even though they did not have knowledge on these topics. These people have helped me to to make the book as it now lies in front of you.

About the Reviewer

Matthew Hill is a British software developer with substantial experience in web application development. An established developer in the TypeScript and JavaScript spheres, he thoroughly enjoys working on open source projects and dipping into often esoteric technologies. Outside of programming, Matthew has a fervent interest in literature.

After graduating with a computer science degree, he started his career at Sky UK Ltd, where he developed video streaming applications, subsequently moving on to engineer single-page analytics applications at payments startup Velocity. Now he's working at financial services leader Tradeweb, fleshing out their next-generation JavaScript-based trading platform.

www.PacktPub.com

For support files and downloads related to your book, please visit www.PacktPub.com.

Did you know that Packt offers eBook versions of every book published, with PDF and ePub files available? You can upgrade to the eBook version at www.PacktPub.com and as a print book customer, you are entitled to a discount on the eBook copy. Get in touch with us at service@packtpub.com for more details.

At www.PacktPub.com, you can also read a collection of free technical articles, sign up for a range of free newsletters and receive exclusive discounts and offers on Packt books and eBooks.

https://www2.packtpub.com/books/subscription/packtlib

Do you need instant solutions to your IT questions? PacktLib is Packt's online digital book library. Here, you can search, access, and read Packt's entire library of books.

Why subscribe?

- Fully searchable across every book published by Packt
- Copy and paste, print, and bookmark content
- On demand and accessible via a web browser

Free access for Packt account holders

If you have an account with Packt at www.PacktPub.com, you can use this to access PacktLib today and view 9 entirely free books. Simply use your login credentials for immediate access.

Table of Contents

Preface

TypeScript allows developers to write readable and maintainable web applications. Editors can provide several tools to the developer, based on types and static analysis of the code. In this book, you will learn how you can use TypeScript to build clean web applications. You will learn how to use Angular 2 and React.

You will also learn how you can use TypeScript for servers, mobile apps, command-line tools, and games. We will build various servers, write a mobile app, rewrite Pac Man, and build Tic-Tac-Toe as a command-line application. You will also learn functional programming. This style of programming will improve your general code skills. You will see how this style can be used in TypeScript.

What this book covers

The book can be divided in two sections. The first section, chapters *1 to 4*, describe how you can build standard application. These chapters introduce Angular 2 and React for web applications, NodeJS for servers and NativeScript for mobile apps. You should read chapters *1 to 3* in a sequence.

The second section, chapters *5 to 8*, introduce more complex concepts. You will learn functional programming in chapters *5 to 7*. The last chapter contains guidance to migrate a JavaScript codebase to TypeScript. You can read chapters *5 to 7* when you have not read chapters *1 to 4*, though chapter *5* requires some knowledge of React.

Chapter 1, *TypeScript 2.0 Fundamentals*, will explain core principals to create (web) applications with TypeScript. If you have some basic knowledge of TypeScript 2.0 then you can skim over this chapter or use it as a reference while reading the other chapters. If you have not used TypeScript yet, then this chapter will teach you the fundamentals of TypeScript 2.0

Chapter 2, *A Weather Forecast Widget with Angular 2*, you will learn how you can build an application in Angular 2. The chapter introduces core principals of Angular and will use an online API as source for the weather forecast.

Chapter 3, *Note-Taking App with a Server*, we will build a server and client with Node and Angular for this application. You will see how code can be shared between the client and the server.

`Chapter` 4, *Real-Time Chat,* introduces React and websockets. Using these techniques, we will write the server and client of the chat application.

`Chapter` 5, *Native QR Scanner App,* after having written three web applications, we will now write a mobile app. You will learn how you can use NativeScript and its plugins to write a native app.

`Chapter` 6, *Advanced Programming in TypeScript,* covers more advanced features of TypeScript, including type guards, control flow analysis and performance of algorithms.

`Chapter` 7, *Spreadsheet Applications with Functional Programming,* introduces a different programming style: functional programming. You will learn how this can be used in TypeScript. We will use React with a Flux-based architecture, which fits nicely with TypeScript and Functional Programming.

`Chapter` 8, *Pac Man in HTML5,* will show how to use the HTML5 canvas to create a game. We will use some Functional Programming again, and take a look at how we can create a framework for it based on the Flux architecture.

`Chapter` 9, *Playing Tic-Tac-Toe against an AI,* will explain how to build a command-line application in which you can play Tic-Tac-Toe. You will learn how you can learn the computer to play the game. When done correctly, the computer should never lose.

`Chapter` 10, *Migrate JavaScript to TypeScript,* will show how you can incrementally migrate a JavaScript codebase to TypeScript. We will focus on how you can keep the project working during this transition.

What you need for this book

You will need an editor to write the code, a terminal to compile the code, and a browser to see the results. Visual Studio Code and Atom with atom-typescript are good editors in which you can write TypeScript code. These are available for Windows, Mac, and Linux. You have to compile TypeScript in a terminal. On Windows, you can use the Command Prompt or Powershell for that. On a Mac, you can use Terminal.

To compile TypeScript, you need NodeJS. You can find details on how you can install it in the first chapter.

`Chapter` 5, *Native QR Scanner App,* has more requirements to run the mobile app in an emulator or a device. Details about how you can install these dependencies are found in the chapter.

Who this book is for

If you are interested in building fun projects using TypeScript, then this book is for you. This book will appeal to web developers who wish to make the most of TypeScript. You should be familiar with the fundamentals of JavaScript.

Conventions

In this book, you will find a number of text styles that distinguish between different kinds of information. Here are some examples of these styles and an explanation of their meaning.

Code words in text, database table names, folder names, filenames, file extensions, pathnames, dummy URLs, user input, and Twitter handles are shown as follows: "We can include other contexts through the use of the `include` directive."

A block of code is set as follows:

```
export function factorial(x: number): number {
   if (x <= 1) return 1;
   return x * factorial(x - 1);
}
```

When we wish to draw your attention to a particular part of a code block, the relevant lines or items are set in bold:

```
export function factorial(x: number): number {
   if (x <= 1) return 1;
   return x * factorial(x - 1);
}
```

Any command-line input or output is written as follows:

```
npm init -y
```

New terms and **important words** are shown in bold.

 Warnings or important notes appear in a box like this.

 Tips and tricks appear like this.

Reader feedback

Feedback from our readers is always welcome. Let us know what you think about this book—what you liked or disliked. Reader feedback is important for us as it helps us develop titles that you will really get the most out of.

To send us general feedback, simply e-mail feedback@packtpub.com, and mention the book's title in the subject of your message.

If there is a topic that you have expertise in and you are interested in either writing or contributing to a book, see our author guide at www.packtpub.com/authors.

Customer support

Now that you are the proud owner of a Packt book, we have a number of things to help you to get the most from your purchase.

Downloading the example code

You can download the example code files for this book from your account at http://www.packtpub.com. If you purchased this book elsewhere, you can visit http://www.packtpub.com/support and register to have the files e-mailed directly to you.

You can download the code files by following these steps:

1. Log in or register to our website using your e-mail address and password.
2. Hover the mouse pointer on the **SUPPORT** tab at the top.
3. Click on **Code Downloads & Errata**.
4. Enter the name of the book in the **Search** box.
5. Select the book for which you're looking to download the code files.
6. Choose from the drop-down menu where you purchased this book from.
7. Click on **Code Download**.

Once the file is downloaded, please make sure that you unzip or extract the folder using the latest version of:

- WinRAR / 7-Zip for Windows
- Zipeg / iZip / UnRarX for Mac
- 7-Zip / PeaZip for Linux

The code bundle for the book is also hosted on GitHub at `https://github.com/PacktPublishing/TypeScript-Blueprints`. We also have other code bundles from our rich catalog of books and videos available at `https://github.com/PacktPublishing/`. Check them out!

Downloading the color images of this book

We also provide you with a PDF file that has color images of the screenshots/diagrams used in this book. The color images will help you better understand the changes in the output. You can download this file from `http://www.packtpub.com/sites/default/files/downloads/TypeScriptBlueprints_ColorImages.pdf`.

Errata

Although we have taken every care to ensure the accuracy of our content, mistakes do happen. If you find a mistake in one of our books-maybe a mistake in the text or the code-we would be grateful if you could report this to us. By doing so, you can save other readers from frustration and help us improve subsequent versions of this book. If you find any errata, please report them by visiting `http://www.packtpub.com/submit-errata`, selecting your book, clicking on the **Errata Submission Form** link, and entering the details of your errata. Once your errata are verified, your submission will be accepted and the errata will be uploaded to our website or added to any list of existing errata under the Errata section of that title.

To view the previously submitted errata, go to https://www.packtpub.com/books/content/support and enter the name of the book in the search field. The required information will appear under the **Errata** section.

Piracy

Piracy of copyrighted material on the Internet is an ongoing problem across all media. At Packt, we take the protection of our copyright and licenses very seriously. If you come across any illegal copies of our works in any form on the Internet, please provide us with the location address or website name immediately so that we can pursue a remedy.

Please contact us at copyright@packtpub.com with a link to the suspected pirated material.

We appreciate your help in protecting our authors and our ability to bring you valuable content.

Questions

If you have a problem with any aspect of this book, you can contact us at questions@packtpub.com, and we will do our best to address the problem.

1

TypeScript 2.0 Fundamentals

In Chapters 2 through 5, we will learn a few frameworks to create (web) applications with TypeScript. First you need some basic knowledge of **TypeScript 2.0**. If you have used TypeScript previously, then you can skim over this chapter, or use it as a reference while reading the other chapters. If you have not used TypeScript yet, then this chapter will teach you the fundamentals of TypeScript.

What is TypeScript?

The TypeScript language looks like JavaScript; it is JavaScript with type annotations added to it. The TypeScript compiler has two main features: it is a **transpiler** and a **type checker**. A transpiler is a special form of compiler that outputs source code. In case of the TypeScript compiler, TypeScript source code is compiled to JavaScript code. A type checker searches for contradictions in your code. For instance, if you assign a string to a variable, and then use it as a number, you will get a type error.

The compiler can figure out some types without type annotations; for others you have to add type annotations. An additional advantage of these types is that they can also be used in editors. An editor can provide completions and refactoring based on the type information. Editors such as Visual Studio Code and Atom (with a plugin, namely atom-typescript) provide such features.

Quick example

The following example code shows some basic TypeScript usage. If you understand this code, you have enough knowledge for the next chapters. This example code creates an input box in which you can enter a name. When you click on the button, you will see a personalized greeting:

```
class Hello {
  private element: HTMLDivElement;
  private elementInput: HTMLInputElement;
  private elementText: HTMLDivElement;
  constructor(defaultName: string) {
    this.element = document.createElement("div");
    this.elementInput = document.createElement("input");
    this.elementText = document.createElement("div");
    const elementButton = document.createElement("button");

    elementButton.textContent = "Greet";

    this.element.appendChild(this.elementInput);
    this.element.appendChild(elementButton);
    this.element.appendChild(this.elementText);

    this.elementInput.value = defaultName;
    this.greet();

    elementButton.addEventListener("click",
      () => this.greet()
    );
  }

  show(parent: HTMLElement) {
    parent.appendChild(this.element);
  }

  greet() {
    this.elementText.textContent = `Hello,
    ${ this.elementInput.value }!`;
  }
}

const hello = new Hello("World");
hello.show(document.body);
```

Downloading the example code

You can download the example code files for this book from your account at `http://www.packtpub.com`. If you purchased this book elsewhere, you can visit `http://www.packtpub.com/support` and register to have the files e-mailed directly to you.

You can download the code files by following these steps:

1. Log in or register to our website using your e-mail address and password.
2. Hover the mouse pointer on the **SUPPORT** tab at the top.
3. Click on **Code Downloads & Errata**.
4. Enter the name of the book in the **Search** box.
5. Select the book for which you're looking to download the code files.
6. Choose from the drop-down menu where you purchased this book from.
7. Click on **Code Download**.

You can also download the code files by clicking on the **Code Files** button on the book's web page at the Packt Publishing website. This page can be accessed by entering the book's name in the **Search** box. Please note that you need to be logged in to your Packt account.

Once the file is downloaded, please make sure that you unzip or extract the folder using the latest version of:

- WinRAR / 7-Zip for Windows
- Zipeg / iZip / UnRarX for Mac
- 7-Zip / PeaZip for Linux

The code bundle for the book is also hosted on GitHub at `https://github.com/PacktPublishing/TypeScript_Blueprints`. We also have other code bundles from our rich catalog of books and videos available at `https://github.com/PacktPublishing/`. Check them out!

The preceding code creates a class, `Hello`. The class has three properties that contain an HTML element. We create these elements in the constructor. TypeScript has different types for all HTML elements and `document.createElement` gives the corresponding element type. If you replace `div` with `span` (on the first line of the constructor), you would get a type error saying that type `HTMLSpanElement` is not assignable to type `HTMLDivElement`. The class has two functions: one to add the element to the HTML page and one to update the greeting based on the entered name.

It is not necessary to specify types for all variables. The types of the variables `elementButton` and `hello` can be inferred by the compiler.

You can see this example in action by creating a new directory and saving the file as `scripts.ts`. In `index.html`, you must add the following code:

```html
<!DOCTYPE HTML>
<html>
  <head>
    <title>Hello World</title>
  </head>
  <body>
    <script src="scripts.js"></script>
  </body>
</html>
```

The TypeScript compiler runs on NodeJS, which can be installed from `https://nodejs.org`. Afterward, you can install the TypeScript compiler by running `npm install typescript -g` in a console/terminal. You can compile the source file by running `tsc scripts.ts`. This will create the `scripts.js` file. Open `index.html` in a browser to see the result.

The next sections explain the basics of TypeScript in more detail. After reading those sections, you should understand this example fully.

Transpiling

The compiler transpiles TypeScript to JavaScript. It does the following transformations on your source code:

- Remove all type annotations
- Compile new JavaScript features for old versions of JavaScript
- Compile TypeScript features that are not standard JavaScript

We can see the preceding three transformations in action in the next example:

```
enum Direction {
  Left,
  Right,
  Up,
  Down
}
let x: Direction = Direction.Left;
```

TypeScript compiles this to the following:

```
var Direction;
(function (Direction) {
    Direction[Direction["Left"] = 0] = "Left";
    Direction[Direction["Right"] = 1] = "Right";
    Direction[Direction["Up"] = 2] = "Up";
    Direction[Direction["Down"] = 3] = "Down";
})(Direction || (Direction = {}));
var x = Direction.Left;
```

In the last line, you can see that the type annotation was removed. You can also see that `let` was replaced by `var`, since `let` is not supported in older versions of JavaScript. The `enum` declaration, which is not standard JavaScript, was transpiled to normal JavaScript.

Type checking

The most important feature of TypeScript is type checking. For instance, for the following code, it will report that you cannot assign a number to a string:

```
let x: string = 4;
```

In the next sections, you will learn the new features of the latest JavaScript versions. Afterward, we will discuss the basics of the type checker.

Learning modern JavaScript

JavaScript has different versions. Some of these are **ES3**, **ES5**, **ES2015** (also known as **ES6**), and **ES2016**. Recent versions are named after the year in which they were introduced. Depending on the environment for which you write code, some features might be or might not be supported. TypeScript can compile new features of JavaScript to an older version of JavaScript. That is not possible with all features, however.

Recent web browsers support ES5 and they are working on ES2015.

We will first take a look at the constructs that can be transpiled to older versions.

let and const

ES2015 has introduced `let` and `const`. These keywords are alternatives to `var`. These prevent issues with scoping, as `let` and `const` are block scoped instead of function scoped. You can use such variables only within the block in which they were created. It is not allowed to use such variables outside of that block or before its definition. The following example illustrates some dangerous behavior that could be prevented with `let` and `const`:

```
alert(x.substring(1, 2));
var x = "lorem";
for (var i = 0; i < 10; i++) {
  setTimeout(function() {
    alert(i);
  }, 10 * i);
}
```

The first two lines give no error, as a variable declared with `var` can be used before its definition. With `let` or `const`, you will get an error, as expected.

The second part shows 10 message boxes saying 10. We would expect 10 messages saying , 1, 2, and so on up to 9. But, when the callback is executed and `alert` is called, i is already 10, so you see 10 messages saying 10.

When you change the `var` keywords to `let`, you will get an error in the first line and the messages work as expected. The variable i is bound to the loop body. For each iteration, it will have a different value. The for loop is transpiled as follows:

```
var _loop_1 = function(i) {
    setTimeout(function () {
        alert(i);
    }, 10 * i);
};
for (var i = 0; i < 10; i++) {
    _loop_1(i);
}
```

A variable declared with `const` cannot be reassigned, and a variable with `let` can be reassigned. If you reassign a `const` variable, you get a compile error.

Classes

As of ES2015, you can create classes easily. In older versions, you could simulate classes to a certain extent. TypeScript transpiles a class declaration to the old way to simulate a class:

```
class Person {
  age: number;
  constructor(public name: string) {
  }
  greet() {
    console.log("Hello, " + this.name);
  }
}

const person = new Person("World");
person.age = 35;
person.greet();
```

This example is transpiled to the following:

```
var Person = (function () {
    function Person(name) {
        this.name = name;
    }
    Person.prototype.greet = function () {
        console.log("Hello, " + this.name);
    };
    return Person;
}());
var person = new Person("World");
person.age = 35;
person.greet();
```

When you prefix an argument of the constructor with public or private, it is added as a property of the class. Other properties must be declared in the body of the class. This is not per the JavaScript specification, but needed with TypeScript for type information.

Arrow functions

ES6 introduced a new way to create functions. **Arrow functions** are function expressions defined using =>. Such function looks like the following:

```
(x: number, y: boolean): string => {
  statements
}
```

The function expression starts with an argument list, followed by an optional return type, the arrow (=>), and then a block with statements. If the function has only one argument without type annotation and no return type annotation, you may omit the parenthesis: x => { ... }. If the body contains only one `return` statement, without any other statements, you can simplify it to (x: number, y: number) => expression. A function with one argument and only a return statement can be simplified to x => expression.

Besides the short syntax, arrow functions have one other major difference with normal functions. Arrow functions share the value of this and the position where it was defined; this is lexically bound. Previously, you would store the value of this in a variable called _this or self, or you would fix the value using .bind(this). With arrow functions, that is not required any more.

Function arguments

It is possible to add a default value to an argument:

```
function sum(a = 0, b = 0, c = 0) {
  return a + b + c;
}
sum(10, 5);
```

When you call this function with less than three arguments, it will set the other arguments to 0. TypeScript will automatically infer the types of a, b, and c based on their default values, so you do not have to add a type annotation there.

You can also define an optional argument without a default value: function a(x?: number) {}. The argument will then be undefined when it is not provided. This is not standard JavaScript, but only available in TypeScript.

The sum function can be defined even better, with a **rest argument**. At the end of a function, you can add a rest argument:

```
function sum(...xs: number[]) {
  let total = 0;
  for (let i = 0; i < xs.length; i++) total += xs[i];
  return total;
}
sum(10, 5, 2, 1);
```

Array spread

It is easier to create arrays in ES6. You can create an array literal (with brackets), in which you use another array. In the following example, you can see how you can add an item to a list and how you can concatenate two lists:

```
const a = [0, 1, 2];
const b = [...a, 3];
const c = [...a, ...b];
```

A similar feature for object literals will probably be added to JavaScript too.

Destructuring

With **destructuring**, you can easily create variables for properties of an object or elements of an array:

```
const a = { x: 1, y: 2, z: 3 };
const b = [4, 5, 6];

const { x, y, z } = a;
const [u, v, w] = b;
```

The preceding is transpiled to the following:

```
var a = { x: 1, y: 2, z: 3 };
var b = [4, 5, 6];

var x = a.x, y = a.y, z = a.z;
var u = b[0], v = b[1], w = b[2];
```

You can use destructing in an assignment, variable declaration, or argument of a function header.

Template strings

With template strings, you can easily create a string with expressions in it. If you would write "Hello, " + name + "!", you can now write Hello ${ name }!.

New classes

ES2015 has introduced some new classes, including `Map`, `Set`, `WeakMap`, `WeakSet`, and `Promise`. In modern browsers, these classes are already available. For other environments, TypeScript does not automatically add a fallback for these classes. Instead, you should use a **polyfill**, such as es6-shim. Most browsers already support these classes, so in most cases, you do not need a polyfill. You can find information on browser support at `http://caniu se.com`.

Type checking

The compiler will check the types of your code. It has several primitive types and you can define new types yourself. Based on these types, the compiler will warn when a value of a type is used in an invalid manner. That could be using a string for multiplication or using a property of an object that does not exist. The following code would show these errors:

```
let x = "foo";
x * 2;
x.bar();
```

TypeScript has a special type, called `any`, that allows everything; you can assign every value to it and you will never get type errors. The type `any` can be used if you do not have an exact type (`yet`), for instance, because it is a complex type or if it is from a library that was not written in TypeScript. This means that the following code gives no compile errors:

```
let x: any = "foo";
x * 2;
x.bar();
```

In the next sections, we will discover these types and learn how the compiler finds these types.

Primitive types

TypeScript has several primitive types, which are listed in the following table:

Name	Values	Example
boolean	true, false	let x: boolean = true;
string	Any string literal	let x: string = "foo";

number	Any number, including `Infinity`, `-Infinity`, and `NaN`	`let x: number = 42;` `let y: number = NaN;`
Literal types	Literal types can only contain one value	`let x: "foo" = "foo";`
void	Only used for a function that does not return a value	`function a(): void { }`
never	No values	
any	All values	`let x: any = "foo";` `let y: any = true;`

Defining types

You can define your own types in various ways:

Kind	Meaning	Example

Object type	Represents an object, with the specified properties. Properties marked with ? are optional. Objects can also have an indexer (for example, like an array), or call signatures. Object types can be defined inline, with a class or with an interface declaration.	`let x: {`
		`  a: boolean,`
		`  b: string,`
		`  c?: number,`
		`  [i: number]:`
		`string`
		`};`
		`x = {`
		`  a: true, b: "foo"`
		`};`
		`x[0] = "foo";`

Union type	A value is assignable to a union type if it is assignable to one of the specified types. In the example, it should be a string or a number.	`let x: string |`
		`number;`
		`x = "foo";`
		`x = 42;`

Intersection type	A value is assignable to an intersection type if it is assignable to all specified types.	`let x: { a: string }`
		`& { b:   number } =`
		`{ a: "foo", b: 42 };`

Enum type	A special number type, with several values declared. The declared members get a value automatically, but you can also specify a value.	`enum E {`
		`  X,`
		`  Y = 100`
		`}`
		`let a: E = E.X;`

Function type	Represents a function with the specified arguments and return type. Optional and rest arguments can also be specified.	```let f: (x: string, y?: boolean) => number;``` ```let g: (...xs: number[]) => number;```
Tuple type	Multiple values are placed in one, as an array.	```let x: [string, number];``` ```X = ["foo", 42];```

Undefined and null

By default, `undefined` and `null` can be assigned to every type. Thus, the compiler cannot give you a warning when a value can possibly be undefined or null. TypeScript 2.0 has introduced a new mode, called `strictNullChecks`, which adds two new types: `undefined` and `null`. With that mode, you do get warnings in such cases. We will discover that mode in `Chapter 6`, *Advanced Programming in TypeScript*.

Type annotations

TypeScript can infer some types. This means that the TypeScript compiler knows the type, without a type annotation. If a type cannot be inferred, it will default to `any`. In such a case, or in case the inferred type is not correct, you have to specify the types yourself. The common declarations that you can annotate are given in the following table:

Location	Can it be inferred?	Examples
Variable declaration	Yes, based on initializer	```let a: number;``` ```let b = 1;```

Function argument	Yes, based on default value (second example) or when passing the function to a typed variable or function (third example)	```function a(x: number) {}```
		 ```function b(x = 1) {}```
		 ```[1, 2].map(```
		 ``` x => x * 2```
		 ```);```

Function return type	Yes, based on return statements in body	```function a(): number { }```
		 ```(): number => { }```
		 ```function c() {```
		 ``` return 1;```
		 ```}```

| Class member | Yes, based on default value | ```class A {
  x: number;
  y = 0;
}``` |
| Interface member | No | ```interface A {
  x: number;
}``` |

You can set the compiler option `noImplicitAny` to get compiler errors when a type could not be inferred and falls back to `any`. It is advised to use that option always, unless you are migrating a JavaScript codebase to TypeScript. You can read about such migration in `Chapter 10`, *Migrate JavaScript to TypeScript*.

Summary

In this chapter, you discovered the basics of TypeScript. You should now be familiar with the principles of TypeScript and you should understand the code example at the beginning of the chapter. You now have the knowledge to start with the next chapters, in which you will learn two major web frameworks, Angular 2 and React. We will start with Angular 2 in `Chapter 2`, *A Weather Forecast Widget with Angular 2*.

2
A Weather Forecast Widget with Angular 2

In this chapter, we'll create a simple application that shows us the weather forecast. The framework we use, Angular 2, is a new framework written by Google in TypeScript. The application will show the weather of the current day and the next. In the following screenshot, you can see the result. We will explore some key concepts of Angular, such as data binding and directives.

We will build the application in the following steps:

- Using modules
- Setting up the project
- Creating the first component
- Adding conditions to the template
- Showing a forecast
- Creating the forecast components
- The main component

Using modules

We will use **modules** in all applications in this book. Modules (also called external modules and ES2015 modules) are a concept of separating code in multiple files. Every file is a module. Within these modules, you can use variables, functions, and classes (members) exported by other modules and you can make some members visible for other modules. To use other modules, you must import them, and to make members visible, you need to export them. The following example will show some basic usage:

```
// x.ts
import { one, add, Lorem } from './y';
console.log(add(one, 2));

var lorem = new Lorem();
console.log(lorem.name);

// y.ts
export var one = 1;
export function add(a: number, b: number) {
  return a + b;
}
export class Lorem {
  name = "ipsum";
}
```

You can **export** declarations by prefixing them with the `export` keyword or by prefixing them with `export default`. A default export should be imported differently though we will not use such an export as it can be confusing. There are various ways to **import** a file. We have seen the variant that is used most times, `import { a, b, c } from './d'`. The dot and slash mean that the `d.ts` file is located in the same directory. You can use `./x/y` and `../z` to reference a file in a subdirectory or a parent directory. A reference that does not start with a dot can be used to import a library, such as Angular. Another import variant is `import * as e from './d'`. This will import all exports from `d.ts`. These are available as `e.a`, `e.b`, `e` is an object that contains all exports.

To keep code readable and maintainable, it is advisable to use multiple small files instead of one big file.

Setting up the project

We will quickly set up the project before we can start writing. We will use `npm` to manage our dependencies and `gulp` to build our project. These tools are built on `NodeJS`, so it should be installed from nodejs.org.

First of all, we must create a new directory in which we will place all files. We must create a `package.json` file used by `npm`:

```
{
  "name": "weather-widget",
  "version": "1.0.0",
  "private": true,
  "description": ""
}
```

The `package.json` file contains information about the project, such as the name, version, and a description. These fields are used by `npm` when you publish a project on the registry on NPM, which contains a lot of open source projects. We will not publish it there. We set the `private` field to `true`, so we cannot accidentally publish it.

Directory structure

We will separate the TypeScript sources from the other files. The TypeScript files will be added in the `lib` directory. Static files, such as HTML and CSS, will be located in the `static` directory. This directory can be uploaded to a webserver. The compiled sources will be written to `static/scripts`. We first install Angular and some requirements of Angular with `npm`. In a terminal, we run the following command in the root directory of the project:

```
npm install angular2 rxjs es6-shim reflect-metadata zone.js --save
```

The console might show some warnings about unmet peer dependencies. These will probably be caused by a minor version mismatch between Angular and one of its dependencies. You can ignore these warnings.

Configuring TypeScript

TypeScript can be configured using a `tsconfig.json` file. We will place that file in the `lib` directory, as all our files are located there. We specify the `experimentalDecorators` and `emitDecoratorMetadata` options, as these are necessary for Angular:

```
{
  "compilerOptions": {
    "target": "es5",
    "module": "commonjs",
    "experimentalDecorators": true,
    "emitDecoratorMetadata": true,
    "lib": ["es2015", "dom"]
  }
}
```

The `target` option specifies the version of JavaScript of the generated code. Current browsers support `es5`. TypeScript will compile newer JavaScript features, such as classes, to an `es5` equivalent. With the `lib` option, we can specify the version of the JavaScript library. We use the libraries from `es2015`, the version after `es5`. Since these libraries might not be available in all browsers, we will add a polyfill for these features later on. We also include the libraries for the **DOM**, which contains functions such as `document.createElement` and `document.getElementById`.

Building the system

With `gulp`, it is easy to compile a program in multiple steps. For most webapps, multiple steps are needed: compiling TypeScript, bundling modules, and finally minifying all code. In this application, we need to do all of these steps.

Gulp streams source files through a series of plugins. These plugins can (just like gulp itself) be installed using `npm`:

```
npm install gulp --global
npm install gulp gulp-typescript gulp-sourcemaps gulp-uglify small --save-
dev
```

The `--global` flag will install the dependency globally such that you can call gulp from a terminal. The `--save-dev` flag will add the dependency to the `devDependencies` (development dependencies) section of the `package.json` file. Use `--save` to add a runtime dependency.

We use the following plugins for gulp:

- The `gulp-typescript` plugin compiles TypeScript to JavaScript
- The `gulp-uglify` plugin can minify JavaScript files
- The `small` plugin can bundle external modules
- The `gulp-sourcemaps` plugin improves the debugging experience with source maps

We will create two tasks, one that compiles the sources to a development build and another that can create a release build. The development build will have source maps and will not be minified, whereas the release build will be minified without source maps. Minifying takes some time so we do not do that on the debug task. Creating source maps in the release task is possible too, but generating the source map is slow so we will not do that.

We write these tasks in `gulpfile.js` in the root of the project. The second task is the easiest to write, as it only uses one plugin. The task will look like this:

```
var gulp = require('gulp');
var uglify = require('gulp-uglify');

gulp.task('release', ['compile'], function() {
  return gulp.src('static/scripts/scripts.js')
    .pipe(uglify())
    .pipe(gulp.dest('static/scripts'));
});
```

The `gulp.task` call will register a task named `release`, which will take `static/scripts/scripts.js` (which will be created by the compile task), run `uglify` (a tool that minifies JavaScript) on it, and then save it in the same directory again. This task depends on the compile task, meaning that the `compile` task will be run before this one.

The first task, `compile`, is more complicated. The task will transpile TypeScript, and bundle the files with the external libraries.

First, we must load some plugins:

```
var gulp = require('gulp');

var typescript = require('gulp-typescript');var small =
require('small').gulp;var sourcemaps = require('gulp-sourcemaps');

var uglify = require('gulp-uglify');
```

We load the configuration of TypeScript in the `tsconfig.json` file:

```
var tsProject = typescript.createProject('lib/tsconfig.json');
```

Now, we can finally write the task. First, we load all sources and compile them using the TypeScript compiler. After that, we bundle these files (including Angular, stored under `node_modules`, using `small`):

```
gulp.task('compile', function() {
  return gulp.src('lib/**/*.ts')
    .pipe(sourcemaps.init())
    .pipe(typescript(tsProject))
    .pipe(small('index.js', {
        externalResolve: ['node_modules'],
        globalModules: {
            "crypto": {
                    standalone: "undefined"
            }
        }
    }))
    .pipe(sourcemaps.write('.'))
    .pipe(gulp.dest('static/scripts'));
});
gulp.task('release', ['compile'], function() {
    return gulp.src('static/scripts/scripts.js')
          .pipe(uglify())
          .pipe(gulp.dest('static/scripts'));
});

gulp.task('default', ['compile']);
```

This task compiles our project and saves the result as `static/scripts/scripts.js`. The `sourcemaps.init()` and `sourcemaps.write('.')` functions handle the creation of source maps, which will improve the debugging experience.

The HTML file

The main file of our application is the HTML file, `static/index.html`. This file will reference our (compiled) scripts and stylesheet:

```
<!DOCTYPE HTML>
<html>
  <head>
    <title>Weather</title>
    <link rel="stylesheet" href="style.css" />
  </head>
```

```
<body>
  <div id="wrapper">
    <weather-widget>Loading..</weather-widget>
  </div>
  <script src="scripts/index.js" type="text/javascript"></script>
</body>
</html>
```

The `weather-widget` tag will be initialized by Angular. We will add some fancy styles in `static/style.css`:

```css
body {
  font-family: 'Segoe UI', Tahoma, Geneva, Verdana, sans-serif;
  font-weight: 100;
}
h1, h2, h3 {
  font-weight: 100;
  margin: 0;
  padding: 0;
  color: #57BEDE;
}
#wrapper {
  position: absolute;
  left: 0;
  right: 0;
  top: 0;
  width: 450px;
  margin: 10% auto;
}
a:link, a:visited {
  color: #57BEDE;
  text-decoration: underline;
}
a:hover, a:active {
  color: #44A4C2;
}
.clearfix {
  clear: both;
}
```

Creating the first component

Angular is based on components. Components are built with other components and normal HTML tags. Our application will have three components: the forecast page, the about page, and the whole widget. The widget itself, which is referenced in the HTML page, will use the other two widgets.

The widget will show the **About** page in the third tab, as you can see in the following screenshot:

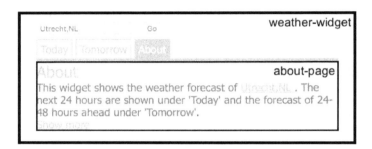

The forecast component is shown in the first tab of the following screenshot. We will create the forecast and the widget later in this chapter.

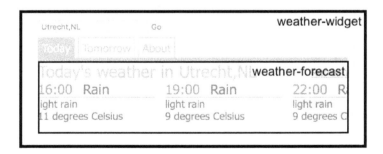

The template

A component is a class decorated with some metadata. **Decorators** are functions that can modify a class or decorate it with some metadata. A simple component that does not have any interaction will look like this:

```
import { Component } from "angular2/core";

@Component({
  selector: "about-page",
template: `
    <h2>About</h2>
    This widget shows the weather forecast of Utrecht.
    The next 24 hours are shown under 'Today' and the forecast of
24-48 hours ahead under 'Tomorrow'.
    `
})
export class About {
}
```

 As a convention, you can always choose selector names with a dash (–). You can then identify components by the dash. Normal HTML tags will never have names with a dash.

This component will be the about page selector of our application. We will modify it in the next sessions. We will use one file per component, so we save this as `lib/about.ts`.

Testing

We can test the component by calling the bootstrap function. We create a new file, `lib/index.ts`, which will start the application:

```
import "zone.js";
import "rxjs";
import "reflect-metadata";
import "es6-shim";
import { bootstrap } from "angular2/platform/browser";
import { About } from "./about";

bootstrap(About).catch(err => console.error(err));
```

The `.catch` section will show errors in the console. If you do not include that call, you will not see those errors and that can be pretty frustrating.

We must change the `weather-widget` tag in `static/index.html` to an `about-page` tag. Now, we can run `gulp` and open `index.html` in a browser to see the results.

At the time of writing this, when you run this command, you get an error when saying that the type definition of `zone.js` is incorrect. You can ignore this error as it is a bug of `zone.js`.

Test early

It's always a good idea to test during development. If you test after writing a lot of code, you will discover issues late, and it will take more work to repair them. Every time that you want to test the project, you must first run `gulp` and then open or refresh `index.html`.

Interactions

We can add an interaction inside the class body. We must use bindings to connect the template to definitions in the body. There are three different bindings:

- One-way variable binding
- One-way event listener
- Two-way binding

A one-way binding will connect the class body and template in one direction. In case of a variable, changes of the variable will update the template, but the template cannot update the variable. A template can only send an event to the class. In case of a two-way binding, a change of the variable changes the template and a change in the template will change the variable. This is useful for the value of an input element, for example. We will take a look at one-way bindings in the next section.

One-way variable binding

In the first attempt of the about page, the location (Utrecht) is hardcoded. In the final application, we want to choose our own location. The first step we will take is to add a property to the class that contains the location. Using a one-way binding, we will reference that value in the template. A one-way variable binding is denoted with brackets inside attributes and double curly brackets inside text:

```
import { Component } from "angular2/core";

@Component({
  selector: "about-page",
  template: `
    <h2>About</h2>
    This widget shows the weather forecast of
    <a [href]="'https://maps.google.com/?q=' + encodedLocation">
      {{ location }}
    </a>
    The next 24 hours are shown under 'Today' and the forecast        of
24-48 hours ahead under 'Tomorrow'.
    `
})
export class About {
  location = "Utrecht";

  get encodedLocation() {
    return encodeURIComponent(this.location);
  }
}
```

At the time of writing this, templates aren't checked by TypeScript. Make sure that you write the correct names of the variables. Variables should not be prefixed by `this.`, like you would do in class methods.

You can add an expression in such bindings. In this example, the binding of the `href` attribute does string concatenation. However, the subset of expressions is limited. You can add more complex code inside getters in the class, as done with `encodedLocation`.

You can also use a different getter, which would encode the location and concatenate it with the Google Maps URL.

Event listeners

Event bindings can connect an event emitter of a tag or component to a method of a function. Such binding is denoted with parenthesis in the template. We will add a show-more button to our application:

```
import { Component} from "angular2/core";

@Component({
  selector: "about-page",
  template: `
    <h2>About</h2>
    This widget shows the weather forecast of
    <a [href]="'https://maps.google.com/?q=' + encodedLocation">
      {{ location }}
    </a>.
    The next 24 hours are shown under 'Today' and the forecast        of
24-48 hours ahead under 'Tomorrow'.
    <br />
    <a href="javascript:;" (click)="show()">Show more</a>
    <a href="javascript:;" (click)="hide()">Show less</a>
    `
})
export class About {
  location = "Utrecht";
  collapsed = true;
  show() {
    this.collapsed = false;
  }
  hide()
  {
    this.collapsed = true;
  }

  get encodedLocation() {
    return encodeURIComponent(this.location);
  }
}
```

The show() or hide() function will be called when one of the show or hide links is clicked on.

Adding conditions to the template

The event handler in the previous section sets the property collapsed to false but that does not modify the template. In normal code, we would have written if (this.collapsed) { ... }. In templates, we cannot use that, but we can use ngIf.

Directives

A directive is an extension to normal HTML tags and attributes. It can define custom behavior. A custom component, such as the **About** page, can be seen as a directive too. The ngIf condition is a built-in directive in Angular. It is a custom attribute that displays the content if the specified value is true.

The template tag

If a piece of a component needs to be shown a variable an amount of times, you can wrap it in a template tag. Using the ngIf (or ngFor) directive, you can control how often it is shown (in case of ngIf, once or zero times). The template tag will look like this:

```
<template [ngIf]="collapsed">
  <div>Content</div>
</template>
```

You can abbreviate this as follows:

```
<div *ngIf="collapsed">Content</div>
```

It is advised to use the abbreviated style, but it's good to remember that it is shorthand for the template tag.

Modifying the about template

Since `ngIf` is a built-in directive, it doesn't have to be imported. Custom directives need to be imported. We will see an example of using custom components later in this chapter. In the template, we can use `*ngIf` now. The template will thus look like this:

```
template: `
  <h2>About</h2>
  This widget shows the weather forecast of
  <a [href]="'https://maps.google.com/?q=' + encodedLocation">
    {{ location }}
  </a>.
  The next 24 hours are shown under 'Today' and the forecast        of
24-48 hours ahead under 'Tomorrow'.
  <br />
  <a *ngIf="collapsed" href="javascript:;" (click)="show()">Show
  more</a>
  <div *ngIf="!collapsed">
  The forecast uses data from <a
  href="http://openweathermap.org">Open Weather Map</a>.
    <br />
    <a href="javascript:;" (click)="hide()">Hide</a>
  </div>
`
})
```

The class body does not have to be changed. As you can see, you can use expressions in the `*ngIf` bindings, which is not surprising as it is a shorthand for one-way variable bindings.

Using the component in other components

We can use the `about-page` component in other components, as if it was a normal HTML tag. But the component is still boring, as it will always say that it shows the weather broadcast of Utrecht. We can mark the `location` property as an input. After that, `location` is an attribute that we can set from other components. It is even possible to bind it as a one-way binding. The `Input` decorator, which we are using here, needs to be imported just like `Component`:

```
import { Component, Input } from "angular2/core";

@Component({
  ...
})
export class About {
```

```
@Input()
location: string = "Utrecht";
collapsed = true;
show() {
  this.collapsed = false;
}
hide() {
  this.collapsed = true;
}

get encodedLocation() {
  return encodeURIComponent(this.location);
}
}
```

Showing a forecast

We still have not shown a forecast yet. We will use data from open weather map (http://www.openweathermap.org). You can create an account on their website. With your account, you can request an API token. You need the token to request the forecast. A free account is limited to 60 requests per second and 50,000 requests per day.

We save the API token in a separate file, lib/config.ts:

```
export const openWeatherMapKey = "your-token-here";
export const apiURL = "http://api.openweathermap.org/data/2.5/";
```

Add constants to a separate file
When you add constants in separate configuration files, you can easily change them and your code is more readable. This gives you better maintainable code.

Using the API

We will create a new file, lib/api.ts, that will simplify downloading data from open weather map. The API uses URLs such as http://api.openweathermap.org/data/2.5/forecast?mode=json&q=Utrecht,NL&appid=your-token-here. We will create a function that will build the full URL out of forecast?mode=json&q=Utrecht,NL. The function must check whether the path already contains a question mark. If so, it must add &appid=, otherwise ?appid=:

```
import { openWeatherMapKey, apiURL } from "./config";
```

```
export function getUrl(path: string) {
  let url = apiURL + path;
  if (path.indexOf("?") === -1) {
    url += "?";
  } else {
    url += "&";
  }
  url += "appid=" + openWeatherMapKey;
  return url;
}
```

Write small functions

Small functions are easy to reuse. This reduces the amount of code you need to write. The same applies to components—small components are easy to reuse.

Typing the API

You can open the URL in the previous section to get a look at the data you get. We will write an interface for the part of the API that we will use:

```
export interface ForecastResponse {
  city: {
    name: string;
    country: string;
  };
  list: ForecastItem[];
}
export interface ForecastItem {
  dt: number;
  main: {
    temp: number
  };
  weather: {
    main: string,
    description: string
  };
}
```

JSDoc comments

You can add documentation for interfaces and their properties by adding a JSDoc comment before it:

```
/*** Documentation here */
```

Creating the forecast component

As a quick recap, the forecast widget will look like this:

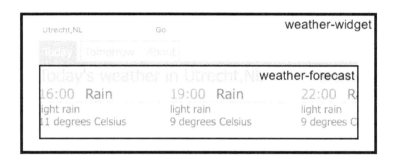

What properties does the class need? The template will need forecast data of the current day or the next day. The component can show the weather of **Today** and **Tomorrow**, so we will also need a property for that. For fetching the forecast, we also need the location. To show the loading state in the template, we will also store that in the class. This will result in the following class, in `lib/forecast.ts`:

```
import { Component, Input } from "angular2/core";
import { ForecastResponse } from "./api";

export interface ForecastData {
  date: string;
  temperature: number;
  main: string;
  description: string;
}

enum State {
  Loading,
  Refreshing,
  Loaded,
  Error
}

@Component({
  selector: "weather-forecast",
  template: `...`
})
export class Forecast {
  temperatureUnit = "degrees Celsius";
```

```
    @Input()
    tomorrow = false;
    @Input()
    location = "Utrecht";

data: ForecastData[] = [];

    state = State.Loading;
}
```

Testing
You can test this component by adjusting the tag in index.html and bootstrapping the right component in index.ts. Run gulp to compile the sources and open the web browser.

Templates

The template uses the ngFor directive to iterate over the data array:

```
import { Component, Input } from "angular2/core";
import { ForecastResponse } from "./api";

...

@Component({
  selector: "weather-forecast",
  template: `
    <span *ngIf="loading" class="state">Loading...</span>
    <span *ngIf="refreshing" class="state">Refreshing...</span>
    <a *ngIf="loaded || error" href="javascript:;"        (click)="load()"
class="state">Refresh</a>
    <h2>{{ tomorrow ? 'Tomorrow' : 'Today' }}'s weather in {{
location }}</h2>
    <div *ngIf="error">Failed to load data.</div>
    <ul>
      <li *ngFor="#item of data">
        <div class="item-date">{{ item.date }}</div>
        <div class="item-main">{{ item.main }}</div>
        <div class="item-description">{{ item.description }}</div>
        <div class="item-temperature">
          {{ item.temperature }} {{ temperatureUnit }}
        </div>
      </li>
    </ul>
    <div class="clearfix"></div>
    `,
```

Using the `styles` property, we can add nice CSS styles, as shown here:

```
styles: [
  `.state {
    float: right;
    margin-top: 6px;
  }
  ul {
    margin: 0;
    padding: 0 0 15px;
    list-style: none;
    width: 100%;
    overflow-x: scroll;
    white-space: nowrap;
  }
  li {
    display: inline-block;
    margin-right: 15px;
    width: 170px;
    white-space: initial;
  }
  .item-date {
    font-size: 15pt;
    color: #165366;
    margin-right: 10px;
    display: inline-block;
  }
  .item-main {
    font-size: 15pt;
    display: inline-block;
  }
  .item-description {
    border-top: 1px solid #44A4C2;
    width: 100%;
    font-size: 11pt;
  }
  .item-temperature {
    font-size: 11pt;
  }`
  ]
})
```

In the `class` body, we add the getters which we used in the template:

```
export class Forecast {
  ...
  state = State.Loading;
  get loading() {
```

```
      return this.state === State.Loading;
    }
    get refreshing() {
      return this.state === State.Refreshing;
    }
    get loaded() {
      return this.state === State.Loaded;
    }
    get error() {
      return this.state === State.Error;
    }
    ...
}
```

Enums
Enums are just numbers with names attached to them. It's more readable to write State.Loaded than 2, but they mean the same in this context.

As you can see, the syntax of ngFor is *ngFor="#variable of array". The enum cannot be referenced from the template, so we need to add getters in the body of the class.

Downloading the forecast

To download data from the Internet in Angular, we need to get the HTTP service. We need to set the viewProviders section for that:

```
import { Component, Input } from "angular2/core";
import { Http, Response, HTTP_PROVIDERS } from "angular2/http";
import { getUrl, ForecastResponse } from "./api";

...

@Component({
  selector: "weather-forecast",
  viewProviders: [HTTP_PROVIDERS],
  template: `...`,
  styles: [...]
})
export class Forecast {
  constructor(private http: Http) {

  }
...
```

Angular will inject the `Http` service into the constructor.

> By including `private` or `public` before an argument of the constructor, that argument will become a property of the class, initialized by the value of the argument.

We will now implement the `load` function, which will try to download the forecast on the specified location. The function can also use coordinates as a location, written as `Coordinates lat lon`, where `lat` and `lon` are the coordinates as shown here:

```
private load() {
  let path = "forecast?mode=json&";
  const start = "coordinate ";
  if (this.location &&
                    this.location.substring(0,
                    start.length).toLowerCase() === start) {
    const coordinate = this.location.split(" ");
    path += `lat=${ parseFloat(coordinate[1]) }&lon=${
parseFloat(coordinate[2]) }`;
  } else {
    path += "q=" + this.location;
  }

  this.state = this.state === State.Loaded ?
        State.Refreshing : State.Loading;
  this.http.get(getUrl(path))
    .map(response => response.json())
    .subscribe(res =>
            this.update(<ForecastResponse> res), ()
            =>this.showError());
  };
```

Three kinds of variables

You can define variables with `const`, `let`, and `var`. A variable declared with `const` cannot be modified. Variables declared with `const` or `let` are block-scoped and cannot be used before their definition. A variable declared with `var` is function scoped and can be used before its definition. Such variable can give unexpected behavior, so it's advised to use `const` or `let`.

The function will first calculate the **URL**, then set the state and finally fetch the data and get returns an observable. An observable, comparable to a promise, is something that contains a value that can change later on. Like with arrays, you can map an observable to a different observable. Subscribe registers a callback, which is called when the observable is changed.

This observable changes only once, when the data is loaded. If something goes wrong, the second callback will be called.

Lambda expressions (inline functions)
The fat arrow (=>) creates a new function. It's almost equal to a function defined with the function keyword (function () { return ... }), but it is scoped lexically, which means that this refers to the value of this outside the function. x => expression is a shorthand for (x) => expression, which is a shorthand for (x) => { return expression; }. TypeScript will automatically infer the type of the argument based on the signature of map and subscribe.

As you can see, this function uses the update and showError functions. The update function stores the results of the open weather map API, and showError is a small function that sets the state to State.Error. Since temperatures of the API are expressed in Kelvin, we must substract 273 to get the value in Celsius:

```
fullData: ForecastData[] = [];
data: ForecastData[] = [];

private formatDate(date: Date) {
  return date.getHours() + ":"
          + date.getMinutes() + ":"
          + date.getSeconds();
}
private update(data: ForecastResponse) {
  if (!data.list) {
    this.showError();
    return;
  }

  this.fullData = data.list.map(item => ({
    date: this.formatDate(new Date(item.dt * 1000)),
    temperature: Math.round(item.main.temp - 273),
    main: item.weather[0].main,
    description: item.weather[0].description
  }));
  this.filterData();
  this.state = State.Loaded;
}
private showError() {
  this.data = [];
  this.state = State.Error;
}
private filterData() {
  const start = this.tomorrow ? 8 : 0;
```

```
    this.data = this.fullData.slice(start, start + 8);
  }
```

The `filterData` method will filter the forecast based on whether we want to see the forecast of today or tomorrow. Open weather map has one forecast per 3 hours, so 8 per day. The `slice` function will return a section of the array. `fullData` will contain the full forecast, so we can easily show the forecast of tomorrow, if we have already shown today.

Change detection
Angular will automatically reload the template when some property is changed, there's no need to invalidate anything (as C# developers might expect). This is called change detection.

We also want to refresh data when the location is changed. If tomorrow is changed, we do not need to download any data, because we can just use a different section of the `fullData` array. To do that, we will use getters and setters. In the setter, we can detect changes:

```
private _tomorrow = false;
@Input()
set tomorrow(value) {
  if (this._tomorrow === value) return;
  this._tomorrow = value;
  this.filterData();
}
get tomorrow() {
  return this._tomorrow;
}


private _location: string;
@Input()
set location(value) {
  if (this._location === value) return;
  this._location = value;
  this.state = State.Loading;
  this.data = [];
  this.load();
}
get location() {
  return this._location;
}
```

Adding @Output

The response of Open weather map contains the name of the city. We can use this to simulate completion later on. We will create an event emitter. Other components can listen to the event and update the location when the event is triggered. The whole code will look like this with final changes highlighted:

```
import { Component, Input, Output, EventEmitter } from "angular2/core";
import { Http, Response, HTTP_PROVIDERS } from "angular2/http";
import { getUrl, ForecastResponse } from "./api";

interface ForecastData {
  date: string;
  temperature: number;
  main: string;
  description: string;
}

enum State {
  Loading,
  Refreshing,
  Loaded,
  Error
}

@Component({
  selector: "weather-forecast",
  viewProviders: [HTTP_PROVIDERS],
  template: `
    <span *ngIf="loading" class="state">Loading...</span>
    <span *ngIf="refreshing" class="state">Refreshing...</span>
    <a *ngIf="loaded || error" href="javascript:;"        (click)="load()"
class="state">Refresh</a>
    <h2>{{ tomorrow ? 'Tomorrow' : 'Today' }}'s weather in {{
location }}</h2>
    <div *ngIf="error">Failed to load data.</div>
    <ul>
      <li *ngFor="#item of data">
        <div class="item-date">{{ item.date }}</div>
        <div class="item-main">{{ item.main }}</div>
        <div class="item-description">{{ item.description }}</div>
        <div class="item-temperature">
          {{ item.temperature }} {{ temperatureUnit }}
        </div>
      </li>
    </ul>
    <div class="clearfix;"></div>
```

```
    `,
  styles: [
    `.state {
      float: right;
      margin-top: 6px;
    }
    ul {
      margin: 0;
      padding: 0 0 15px;
      list-style: none;
      width: 100%;
      overflow-x: scroll;
      white-space: nowrap;
    }
    li {
      display: inline-block;
      margin-right: 15px;
      width: 170px;
      white-space: initial;
    }
    .item-date {
      font-size: 15pt;
      color: #165366;
      margin-right: 10px;
      display: inline-block;
    }
    .item-main {
      font-size: 15pt;
      display: inline-block;
    }
    .item-description {
    border-top: 1px solid #44A4C2;
      width: 100%;
      font-size: 11pt;
    }
    .item-temperature {
      font-size: 11pt;
    }`
  ]
})
export class Forecast {
  constructor(private http: Http) {

  }

  temperatureUnit = "degrees Celsius";

  private _tomorrow = false;
```

```
@Input()
set tomorrow(value) {
  if (this._tomorrow === value) return;
  this._tomorrow = value;
  this.filterData();
}
get tomorrow() {
  return this._tomorrow;
}

private _location: string;
@Input()
set location(value) {
  if (this._location === value) return;
  this._location = value;
  this.state = State.Loading;
  this.data = [];
  this.load();
}
get location() {
  return this._location;
}

fullData: ForecastData[] = [];
data: ForecastData[] = [];

state = State.Loading;
get loading() {
  return this.state === State.Loading;
}
get refreshing() {
  return this.state === State.Refreshing;
}
get loaded() {
  return this.state === State.Loaded;
}
get error() {
  return this.state === State.Error;
}

@Output()
correctLocation = new EventEmitter<string>(true);

private formatDate(date: Date) {
  return date.getHours() + ":" + date.getMinutes() +
date.getSeconds();
}
private update(data: ForecastResponse) {
```

```
    if (!data.list) {
      this.showError();
      return;
    }

    const location = data.city.name + ", " + data.city.country;
    if (this._location !== location) {
            this._location = location;
            this.correctLocation.next(location);
    }

    this.fullData = data.list.map(item => ({
      date: this.formatDate(new Date(item.dt * 1000)),
      temperature: Math.round(item.main.temp - 273),
      main: item.weather[0].main,
      description: item.weather[0].description
    }));
    this.filterData();
    this.state = State.Loaded;
  }
  private showError() {
    this.data = [];
    this.state = State.Error;
  }
  private filterData() {
    const start = this.tomorrow ? 8 : 0;
    this.data = this.fullData.slice(start, start + 8);
  }

  private load() {
    let path = "forecast?mode=json&";
    const start = "coordinate ";
    if (this.location&&this.location.substring(0,
start.length).toLowerCase() === start) {
      const coordinate = this.location.split(" ");
      path += `lat=${ parseFloat(coordinate[1]) }&lon=${
parseFloat(coordinate[2]) }`;
    } else {
      path += "q=" + this.location;
    }

    this.state = this.state === State.Loaded ? State.Refreshing         :
State.Loading;
    this.http.get(getUrl(path))
      .map(response => response.json()))
      .subscribe(res => this.update(<ForecastResponse> res),           () =>
this.showError());
  }
```

```
}
```

 The generic (type argument) in `new EventEmitter<string>()` means that the contents of an event will be a string. If the generic is not specified, it defaults to `{}`, an empty object type, which means that there is no content. In this case, we want to send the new location, which is a string.

The main component

As you can see in the screenshot in the introduction of this chapter, this component should have a textbox, a button, and three tabs. Under the tabs, these component will show the forecast or the **About page**.

Using our other components

We can use our components that we have already written by adding them to the `directives` section and using their tag names in the template.

Two-way bindings

To get the value of the input box, we need two-way bindings. We can use the `ngModel` directive for that. The syntax combines the syntaxes of the two one-way bindings: `[(ngModel)]="property"`. The directive is again a built-in one, so we don't have to import it.

Using this two-way binding, we can automatically update the weather widget after every key press. That would cause a lot of requests to the server, and especially on slow connections, that's not desired.

To prevent these issues, we will add two separate properties. The property location will contain the content of the input and `activeLocation` will contain the location, which is being shown.

Listening to our event

We can listen to our event, just like we did with other events. We can access the event content with `$event`. Such a listener will look like `(correct-location)="correctLocation($event)`. When the server responds with the forecast, it also provides the name of the location. If the user had a small typo in the name, the response will correct that. This event will be fired in such a case and the name will be corrected in the input box.

Geolocation API

Because our forecast widget supports coordinates, we can use the geolocation API to set the initial location. That API can give the coordinates where the device is located (roughly). Later on, we will use this API to set the widget to the current location when the page loads as shown here:

```
navigator.geolocation.getCurrentPosition(position => {
  const location = `Coordinate ${ position.coords.latitude }      ${
position.coords.longitude }`;
  this.location = location;
  this.activeLocation = location;
});
```

Template string
Template strings, not to be confused with Angular templates, are strings wrapped in backticks (` ` `). These strings can be multiline and can contain expressions between `${` and `}`.

Component sources

As usual, we start by importing Angular. We also have to import the two components we have already written. We use an enumeration again to store the state of the component:

```
import { Component } from "angular2/core";
import { Forecast } from "./forecast";
import { About } from "./about";

enum State {
  Today,
  Tomorrow,
  About
}
```

The template will use the two-way binding on the input element:

```
@Component({
  selector: "weather-widget",
  directives: [Forecast, About],
  template: `
    <input [(ngModel)]="location" (keyup.enter)="clickGo()"
(blur)="clickGo()" />
    <button (click)="clickGo()">Go</button>
    <div class="tabs">
      <a href="javascript:;" [class.selected]="selectedTab === 0"
(click)="selectTab(0)">Today</a>
      <a href="javascript:;" [class.selected]="selectedTab === 1"
(click)="selectTab(1)">Tomorrow</a>
      <a href="javascript:;" [class.selected]="selectedTab === 2"
(click)="selectTab(2)">About</a>
    </div>
    <div class="content" [class.is-dirty]="isDirty"      *ngIf="selectedTab
=== 0 || selectedTab === 1">
      <weather-forecast [location]="activeLocation"
[tomorrow]="selectedTab === 1"
(correctLocation)="correctLocation($event)" />
    </div>
    <div class="content" *ngIf="selectedTab === 2">
      <about-page [location]="activeLocation" />
    </div>
    `,
```

Binding to class.selected means that the element will have the selected class if the bound value is true. After the template, we can add some styles as shown here:

```
styles: [
  `.tabs > a {
    display: inline-block;
    padding: 5px;
    margin-top: 5px;
    border: 1px solid #57BEDE;
    border-bottom: 0px none;
    text-decoration: none;
  }
  .tabs>a.selected {
    background-color: #57BEDE;
    color: #fff;
  }
  .content {
    border-top: 5px solid #57BEDE;
  }
  .is-dirty {
```

```
      opacity: 0.4;
      background-color: #ddd;
    }`
  ]
})
```

In the constructor, we can use the geolocation API to get the coordinates of the current position:

```
export class Widget {
  constructor() {
    navigator.geolocation.getCurrentPosition(position => {
      const location = `Coordinate ${ position.coords.latitude }
${ position.coords.longitude }`;
      this.location = location;
      this.activeLocation = location;
    });
  }

  location: string = "Utrecht,NL";
  activeLocation: string = "Utrecht,NL";
  get isDirty() {
    return this.location !== this.activeLocation;
  }

  clickGo() {
    this.activeLocation = this.location;
  }
  correctLocation(location: string) {
    if (!this.isDirty) this.location = location;
    this.activeLocation = location;
  }

  selectedTab = 0;
  selectTab(index: number) {
    this.selectedTab = index;
  }
}
```

Summary

In this chapter, we created an application with Angular 2. We explored Angular 2 and used its directives and bindings in our components. We also used an online API. You should now be able to build small Angular applications. In the next chapter, we will build a more complex application in Angular, which will also use its own server.

3
Note-Taking App with a Server

In this chapter, we will create a client-server app. The client will be written using **Angular 2** and the server will be written using **NodeJS** and MongoDB. We can use TypeScript on both sides and we will see how we can reuse code between them.

The application can be used to take notes. We will implement a login page and basic ,**Create, Read, Update, and Delete** (**CRUD**) operations for the notes.

My Notes
Log out
New

- Shoppinglist
- Todo

In this chapter, we will cover the following topics:

- Setting up the project structure
- Getting started with NodeJS
- Understanding the structural type system
- Adding authentication
- Testing the API
- Adding CRUD operations
- Writing the client side
- Running the application

Setting up the project structure

First, we have to setup the project. The difference with the previous chapter is that we now have to build two applications—the client side and the server side. This causes some differences with the previous setup.

Directories

We will again place our TypeScript sources in the `lib` directory. In that directory, we will create four subdirectories: `client`, `server`, `shared`, and `typings`. The `lib/client` directory will contain the client-side application and the `lib/server` directory will contain the server code. Codes that can be used by both the server and the client will go in `lib/shared`. Last but not least, `lib/typings` will contain type definitions for some dependencies, including NodeJS.

Configuring the build tool

In `lib`, we create a `tsconfig.json` file that will contain some configuration for TypeScript. We want to compile the server-side code to `es2015`, so we can use some new features of TypeScript and JavaScript. The client side, however, must be compiled to `es5` for browser support. In the `tsconfig` file, we will specify `es2015` as target and override it in the `gulp` file. We can also specify the version of the default library that we want to use. We need es2015 and dom. The first contains the recent classes and functions from JavaScript, such as `Map` and `Object.assign`:

```
{
  "compilerOptions": {
    "target": "es6",
    "module": "commonjs",
    "experimentalDecorators": true,
    "emitDecoratorMetadata": true,
    "lib": ["es2015", "dom"]
  }
}
```

The `lib` option will only make the types for new classes and functions available. At runtime, these might not be present. We include a polyfill, es6-shim, to make sure that these will always be available.

The `gulp` file, located in the root of the project, is comparable to the configuration of the previous chapter. We can install all necessary dependencies, including runtime dependencies, using `npm`:

```
npm init
npm install gulp gulp-typescript small gulp-sourcemaps merge2 gulp-concat gulp-uglify --save-dev
npm install angular2 es6-shim rxjs phaethon --save
```

You can again set the private property in `package.json` so that you don't accidentally upload your project to `npm`. In `gulpfile.js`, we can now load all dependencies:

```
var gulp = require("gulp");
var typescript = require("gulp-typescript");
var small = require("small").gulp;
var sourcemaps = require("gulp-sourcemaps");
var merge = require("merge2");
var concat = require("gulp-concat");
var uglify = require("gulp-uglify");
```

We will create two TypeScript projects: one for the server and one for the client side. In the second project, we will override the target to `es5`:

```
var tsServer = typescript.createProject("lib/tsconfig.json");
var tsClient = typescript.createProject("lib/tsconfig.json", {
  target: "es5"
});
```

Now we can use almost the same task as in the previous chapter. The sources must be loaded from `lib/client` instead of `lib`, and `lib/shared` should be included too:

```
gulp.task("compile-client", function() {
  return gulp.src(["lib/client/**/*.ts", "lib/shared/**/*.ts"],        {
base: "lib" })
    .pipe(sourcemaps.init())
    .pipe(typescript(tsClient))
    .pipe(small('client/index.js', {
      outputFileName: { standalone: "scripts.js" },
      externalResolve: ['node_modules'],
      globalModules: {
        "crypto": {
          standalone: "undefined"
        }
```

```
        }
    }))
    .pipe(sourcemaps.write('.'))
    .pipe(gulp.dest('static/scripts'));
});
```

The compilation of the server-side code is simpler, as the code doesn't have to be bundled. NodeJS has a built-in module loader:

```
gulp.task("compile-server", function() {
    return gulp.src(["lib/server/**/*.ts", "lib/shared/**/*.ts"], { base:
"lib" })
        .pipe(sourcemaps.init())
        .pipe(typescript(tsServer))
        .pipe(sourcemaps.write("."))
        .pipe(gulp.dest("dist"));
});
```

We add the release and default tasks that can build the release and debug tasks:

```
gulp.task("release", ["compile-client", "compile-server"],      function() {
    return gulp.src("static/scripts/scripts.js")
        .pipe(uglify())
        .pipe(gulp.dest("static/scripts"));
});

gulp.task("default", ["compile-client", "compile-server"]);
```

The tasks can be started using `gulp` or `gulp release`.

Type definitions

Before a library can be used in TypeScript, you have to have type definitions for it. These are stored in `.d.ts` files. For some packages, these are automatically installed. For example, we used Angular in the previous chapter and we didn't install the definitions manually. Packages distributed on `npm` can include their type definitions in the same package. When you download such a package, the `typings` come along. Unfortunately, not all packages do this. As of TypeScript 2.0, it is possible to download `typings` for these packages on `npm` too. For instance, the `typings` for `mongodb` are published in the `@types/mongodb` package. You can install types for a lot of packages this way. Types for NodeJS itself are available in `@types/node`. Run these commands in the `root` directory:

```
npm install @types/node --save
npm install @types/mongodb --save
```

The compiler will automatically find the types for `mongodb` when you import it. Since we will not explicitly import NodeJS in the code, the compiler will not find it. We must add it to our `tsconfig` file.

```
{
  "compilerOptions": {
    "target": "es6",
    "module": "commonjs",
    "experimentalDecorators": true,
    "emitDecoratorMetadata": true,
    "lib": ["es2015", "dom"],
    "types": ["node"]
  }
}
```

The compiler can now use all type definitions.

Getting started with NodeJS

In the previous chapter, we used NodeJS, as gulp uses it. Node can be used for a server and for a command line tool. In this chapter, we will build a server and in Chapter 9, *Playing Tic-Tac-Toe against an AI*, we will create a command line application. If you haven't installed Node yet, you can download it from nodejs.org.

We will first create a simple server. We will use **Phaethon**, a package for Node that makes it easy to build a server in NodeJS. Phaethon includes type definitions, so we can use it immediately. We create a file `lib/server/index.ts` and add the following:

```
import { Server } from "phaethon";
const server = new Server();
server.listener = request => new phaethon.ServerResponse("Hello");
server.listenHttp(8800);
```

We can run this server using the following command:

```
gulp && node dist/server
```

When you open `localhost:8800` in a web browser, the listener callback will be called and you will see **Hello** in the browser.

Asynchronous code

A server doesn't do all the work itself. It will also delegate some tasks. For instance, it might need to download a webpage or fetch something from a database. Such a task will not give a result immediately. In the meantime, the server could do something else. This style of programming is called asynchronous or nonblocking, as the order of execution is not fixed and such task does not block the rest of the application.

Imagine we have a task that will download a webpage. The synchronous variant would look like the following:

```
function download() {
  return ...;
}

function demo() {
// Before download
try {
const result = download();
const result2 = download();
// Download completed
} catch (error) {
  // Error
}
}
```

Callback approach for asynchronous code

In a webserver, this would prevent the server from handling other requests. The task blocks the whole server. That is, of course, not what we want. The simplest asynchronous approach uses callbacks. The first argument of the callback will contain an error if something went wrong and the second argument will contain the result if there is a result:

```
function download(callback: (error: any, result: string) => void) {
  ...
}

function demo() {
// Before download
download((error, result) => {
if (error) {
    // Error
  } else {
    // Download completed
    download((error2, result2) => {
```

```
        if (error2) {
          } else {
          // Download 2 completed
          }
      });
    }
  });
}
```

Disadvantages of callbacks

The disadvantage of this is that when you have a lot of callbacks, you have to nest callbacks in callbacks, which is called callback hell. In ES6, a new class was introduced, that acts like an abstraction of such a task. It is called a promise. Such a value promises that there will be a result now or later on. The promise can be resolved, which means that the result is ready. The promise can also be rejected, which means that there was some error:

```
function download(): Promise<string> {
  ...
}

function demo() {
// Before download
download().then(result => {
  // Download completed

  return download();
}).then(result2 => {
  // Second download completed
});
}
```

As you can see, the preceding code is more readable than the callbacks code. It's also easier to chain tasks since you can return another promise in the `then` section of a promise. However, the synchronous code is still more readable. ES7 has introduced **async** functions. These functions are syntactic sugar around promises. Instead of calling `then` on a promise, you can **await** it and write code as if it were synchronous.

 At the time of writing, `async` functions can only be compiled to ES6. TypeScript 2.1 will introduce support for ES5 too.

```
function download(): Promise<string> {
  ...
```

```
}

async function demo() {
 try {
 const result = await download();
 const result2 = await download();
 } catch (error) {
 }
}
```

As you can see, this is almost the same as the code we started with. This gives the best of both worlds: it results in readable and performant code.

 Do not forget the `async` keyword in the function header. If you want to annotate the function with a return type, write `Promise<T>` instead of `T`.

The database

A lot of programmers use MongoDB in combination with NodeJS. You can install MongoDB from `www.mongodb.org`. MongoDB can be started using the following command in the project root:

mongod --dbpath ./data

You can keep the preceding command running in one terminal window and run NodeJS in another terminal window later on.

Wrapping functions in promises

We will run the database on the same computer as the server and we will name the database `notes`. This yields the URL `mongodb://localhost/notes`, which we need to connect to the database. We have already installed the definitions with **tsd**. MongoDB exposes an API based on callbacks. We will wrap these in promises, as we will use async/await later on. Wrapping a function in a promise will look like the following:

```
function wrapped() {
  return new Promise<string>((resolve, reject) => {
    originalFunction((error, result) => {
        if (error) {
          reject(error);
        } else {
```

```
            resolve(result);
        }
      });
  });
}
```

The `Promise` constructor takes a callback function. This function can call the resolve callback if everything succeeded or call the reject function if something failed.

Connecting to the database

We add the following in `lib/server/database.ts`. First we must connect to the database. Instead of rejecting when the connection failed, we will throw the error. This way the server will quit if it can't connect to the database:

```
import { MongoClient, Db, Collection } from "mongodb";

const databaseUrl = "mongodb://localhost:27017/notes";
const database = new Promise<Db>(resolve => {
  MongoClient.connect(databaseUrl, (error, db) => {
    if (error) {
      throw error;
    }
    resolve(db);
  })
});
```

 Usually, you would reject the promise in case of an error. Here, we throw the error and crash the server. In this case it is better since the server cannot do anything without a database connection.

The database contains two collections (tables): `users` and `notes`. Since we can only access these after the connection to the database has succeeded, these should also be placed in a `Promise`. Since `database` already is a `Promise`, we can use `async/await`:

```
async function getCollection(name: string) {
  const db = await database;
  return db.collection(name);
}
export const users = getCollection("users");
export const notes = getCollection("notes");
```

The `users` and `notes` variables have the type `Promise<Collection>`.

We can now write a function that will insert an item into a collection and return a promise. Since this promise doesn't have a resulting value, we will type it as `Promise<void>`:

```
export function insert(table: Promise<Collection>, item: any) {
  const collection = await table;
  return new Promise<void>((resolve, reject) => {
    collection.insertOne(item, (error) => {
      if (error) {
        reject(error);
      } else {
        resolve();
      }
    });
  });
}
```

Querying the database

To query the database, we will use the function `find`. MongoDB returns a cursor object, which allows you to stream all results. If you have a big application, and queries that return a lot of results, this can improve the performance of your application. Instead of streaming the results, we can also buffer them in an array with the `toArray` function:

```
export function find(table: Promise<Collection>, query: any) {
  const collection = await table;
  return new Promise<U[]>((resolve, reject) => {
    collection.find(query, (error, cursor) => {
      if (error) {
        reject(error);
      } else {
        cursor.toArray((error, results) => {
          if (error) {
            reject(error);
          } else {
            resolve(results);
          }
        });
      }
    });
  });
}
```

We will add `update` and `remove` functions later on.

Understanding the structural type system

TypeScript uses a structural type system. What that means can be easily demonstrated using the following example:

```
class Person {
  name: string;
}
class City {
  name: string;
}
const x: City = new Person();
```

In languages like C#, this would not compile. These languages use a nominal type system. Based on the name, a `Person` is not a `City`. TypeScript uses a structural type system. Based on the structure of `Person` and `City`, these types are equal, as they both have a `name` property. This fits well in the dynamic nature of JavaScript. It can, however, lead to some unexpected behavior, as the following would compile:

```
class Foo {
}
const f: Foo = 42;
```

Since `Foo` does not have any properties, every value would be assignable to it. In cases were the structural behavior is not desired, you can add a **brand**, a property that adds type safety but does not exist at runtime:

```
class Foo {
  __fooBrand: void;
}
const f: Foo = 42;
```

Now the last line will give an error, as expected.

Generics

The typings for MongoDB don't use generics or type arguments. Given that we already have to add a tiny wrapper around it, we can also easily add generics to that wrapper. We will create a new type for the data store that has generics:

```
export interface Table<T> extends Collection {
  __tableBrand: T;
}
```

If you din't include the brand, Table<A> would be structurally identical to Table<B>, which we do not want. We can now load the collections with the correct types. We use the User and Note types here. We will create these interfaces later on:

```
import { User } from "./user";
import { Note } from "./note";

async function getCollection<U>(name: string) {
  const db = await database;
  return <Table<U>> db.collection(name);
}
export const users = getCollection<User>("users");
export const notes = getCollection<Note>("notes");
```

With generics, the insert function will look like the following:

```
export function insert<U>(table: Table<U>, item: U) {
  return new Promise<void>((resolve, reject) => {
    table.insertOne(item, (error) => {
      if (error) {
        reject(error);
      } else {
        resolve();
      }
    });
  });
}
```

For find, we want the query to be a supertype of the table content. In other words, you want to query on some properties of the content of the table. Support for this was added in TypeScript 1.8:

```
export function find<U extends V, V>(table: Table<U>, query: V) {
  return new Promise<U[]>((resolve, reject) => {
    table.find(query, (error, result) => {
      if (error) {
        reject(error);
      } else {
        resolve(result);
      }
    });
  });
}
```

We will also write wrappers for update and remove. Together these functions can do the **CRUD** operations: create, read, update, and delete:

```
export function update<U extends V, V>(table: Table<U>, query: V, newItem:
U) {
  return new Promise<void>((resolve, reject) => {
    table.update(query, newItem, (error) => {
      if (error) {
        reject(error);
        } else {
          resolve();
        }
    });
  });
}
export function remove<U extends V, V>(table: Table<U>, query: V) {
  return new Promise<void>((resolve, reject) => {
    table.remove(query, (error) => {
      if (error) {
      reject(error);
      } else {
        resolve();
      }
    });
  });
}
```

In `lib/server/user.ts`, we will create the `User` model. For MongoDB, such types should have an `_id` property. The database will use that property to identify instances of the models:

```
import { ObjectID } from "mongodb";
export interface User {
  _id: ObjectID;
  username: string;
  passwordHash: string;
}
```

And in `lib/server/note.ts`, we add the `Note` model:

```
import { ObjectID } from "mongodb";
export interface Note {
  _id: ObjectID;
  userId: string;
  content: string;
}
```

Typing the API

In `lib/shared/api.ts`, we will add some typings for the API. On the server side, we can check that the response has the right type:

```
export interface LoginResult {
  ok: boolean;
  message?: string;
}
export interface MenuResult {
  items: MenuItem[];
}
export interface MenuItem {
  id: string;
  title: string;
}
export interface ItemResult {
  id: string;
  content: string;
}
```

We will now implement the functions that return these types.

Adding authentication

In `lib/server/index.ts`, we will first add sessions. A session is a place to store data, which is persistent for a client on the server. On the client side, a cookie will be saved, which contains an identifier of the session. If a request contains a valid cookie with such an identifier, you will get the same session object. Otherwise, a new session will be created:

```
import { Server, ServerRequest, ServerResponse, ServerError, StatusCode,
SessionStore } from "phaethon";
import { ObjectID } from "mongodb";
import { User, login, logout } from "./user";
import * as note from "./note";
```

With `import { ... }`, we can import a set of entities from another file. With `import * as ...`, we import the whole file as an object. The following two snippets are equivalent:
`import * as foo from "./foo"; foo.bar(); import { bar }`
`from "./foo"; bar();`

We define the type of the content of the session as follows:

```
export interface Session {
  userId: ObjectID;
}

const server = new Server();
```

The sessions will be stored in a `SessionStore`. The lifetime of a session is `60 * 60 * 24` seconds or one day:

```
const sessionStore = new SessionStore<Session>("session-id", ()    => ({
userId: undefined }), 60 * 60 * 24, 1024);
server.listener = sessionStore.wrapListener(async (request,    session) =>
{
  const response = await handleRequest(request, session.data);
  if (response instanceof ServerResponse) {
    return response;
  } else {
    const serverResponse = new
ServerResponse(JSON.stringify(response));
  return serverResponse;
  }
});
server.listenHttp(8800);
```

`JSON.stringify` will convert an object to a string. Such a string can easily be converted back to an object on the client side. In `Chapter 2`, *Weather Forecast Widget,* the responses of the weather API were also formatted as JSON strings.

In `handleRequest`, all requests will be sent to a handler based on their path:

```
async function handleRequest(request: ServerRequest, session: Session):
Promise<ServerResponse | Object> {
  const path = request.path.toLowerCase();

  if (path === "/api/login") return login(request, session);
  if (path === "/api/logout") return logout(request, session);
  throw new ServerError(StatusCode.ClientErrorNotFound);
}
```

Implementing users in the database

Now we can implement authentication in `user.ts`. For safety, we won't store plain passwords in our database. Instead we **hash** them. A hash is a manipulation of an input, in a way that you cannot find the input based on the hash. When someone wants to log in, the password is hashed and compared with the hashed password from the database. Using the built-in module crypto, this can easily be done:

```
import * as crypto from "crypto";
function getPasswordHash(username: string, password: string):    string {
   return crypto.createHash("sha256").update(password.length + "-"    +
username + "-" + password).digest("hex");
}
```

The `logout` handler is easy to write. We must remove the `userId` of the session as follows:

```
export function logout(request: ServerRequest, session: Session):
LoginResult {
   session.userId = undefined;
   return { ok: true };
}
```

As you can see, we are using the `LoginResult` interface that we wrote previously. The login function will use the `async/await` syntax. The function expects that the username and password are available in the URL query. If they are not available, `validate.expect` will throw an error, which will be displayed as a `Bad Request` error:

```
export async function login(request: ServerRequest, session:    Session):
Promise<LoginResult> {
   const username = validate.expect(request.query["username"],
validate.isString);
   const password = validate.expect(request.query["password"],
validate.isString);
   constpasswordHash = getPasswordHash(username, password);

   const results = await find(users, { username, passwordHash });
   if (results.length === 0) {
     return { ok: false, message: "Username or password incorrect" };
   }
   const user = results[0];
   session.userId = user._id;
   return { ok: true };
}
```

Adding users to the database

To add some users to the database, we must add some code and run the server once with it. In a real-world application, you would probably want to add a register form. That is comparable to adding a note, which we will do later on in this chapter.

We will also add two helper functions that we can use in `note.ts` to check whether the user is logged in:

```
import * as crypto from "crypto";
import { ServerRequest, ServerResponse, ServerError, StatusCode, validate }
from "phaethon";
import { Session } from "./index";
import { LoginResult } from "../shared/api";
import { users, find, insert } from "./database";

export interface User {
  _id: string;
  username: string;
  passwordHash: string;
}

function getPasswordHash(username: string, password: string): string {
  return crypto.createHash("sha256").update(password.length + "-"        +
username + "-" + password).digest("hex");
}

insert(users, {
  _id: undefined,
  username: "lorem",
  passwordHash: getPasswordHash("lorem", "ipsum")
});
insert(users, {
  _id: undefined,
  username: "foo",
  passwordHash: getPasswordHash("foo", "bar")
});

export async function login(request: ServerRequest, session: Session):
Promise<LoginResult> {
  const username = validate.expect(
    request.query["username"], validate.isString);
  const password = validate.expect(
    request.query["password"], validate.isString);
  const passwordHash = getPasswordHash(username, password);

  const results = await find(users, { username, passwordHash });
```

```
    if (results.length === 0) {
      return { ok: false, message: "Username or password incorrect" };
    }
    const user = results[0];
    session.userId = user._id;
    return { ok: true };
  }
  export function logout(request: ServerRequest, session: Session):    Login
Result {
    session.userId = undefined;
    return { ok: true };
  }
  export async function getUser(session: Session) {
    if (session.userId === undefined) return undefined;
    const results = await find(users, { _id: session.userId });
    return results[0];
  }
  export async function getUserOrError(session: Session) {
    const user = await getUser(session);
    if (user === undefined) {
      throw new ServerError(StatusCode.ClientErrorUnauthorized);
    }
    return user;
  }
```

Run the server once and remove the two `insert` calls afterward.

Testing the API

We can start the server by running the following command:

```
gulp && node --harmony_destructuring dist/server
```

In a web browser, you can open
`localhost:8800/api/login?username=lorem&password=ipsum` to test the code. You
can change the parameters to test how a wrong username or password behaves.

For debugging, you can add `console.log("...");` calls in your code.

Adding CRUD operations

Most servers handle CRUD operations primarily. Our server must handle five different requests: `list` all notes of the current user, `find` a specific note, `insert` a new note, `update` a note, and `remove` a note.

First, we add a helper function that can be used on the server side and the client side. In `lib/shared/note.ts`, we add a function that returns the title of a note—the first line, if available, or "Untitled":

```
export function getTitle(content: string) {
  const lineEnd = content.indexOf("\n");
  if (content === "" || lineEnd === 0) {
    return "Untitled";
  }
  if (lineEnd === -1) {
    // Note contains one line
    return content;
  }
  // Get first line
  return content.substring(0, lineEnd);
}
```

We write the CRUD functions in `lib/server/note.ts`. We start with imports and the `Note` definition:

```
import { ServerRequest, ServerResponse, ServerError, StatusCode, validate }
from "phaethon";
import { ObjectID } from "mongodb";
import { Session } from "./index";
import { getUserOrError } from "./user";
import { Note } from "./note";
import { getTitle } from "../shared/note";
import { MenuResult, ItemResult } from "../shared/api";
import * as database from "./database";

export interface Note {
  _id: string;
  userId: string;
  content: string;
}
```

Implementing the handlers

Now we can implement the `list` function. Using the helper functions we wrote previously, we can easily write the following function:

```
export async function list(request: ServerRequest, session: Session):
Promise<MenuResult> {
  const user = await getUserOrError(session);
  const results = await database.find(
    database.notes, { userId: user._id });
  const items = results.map(note => ({
    id: note._id.toHexString(),
    title: getTitle(note.content)
  }));
  return { items };
}
```

With `toHexString`, an `ObjectID` can be converted to a string. It can be converted back using `new ObjectID(...)`. The map function transforms an array with a specific callback.

In the `find` function, we must search for a note based on a specific ID:

```
export async function find(request: ServerRequest, session: Session):
Promise<ItemResult> {
  const user = await getUserOrError(session);
  const id = validate.expect(
    request.query["id"], validate.isString);
  const notes = await database.find(database.notes,
    { _id: new ObjectID(id), userId: user._id });
  if (notes.length === 0) {
    throw new ServerError(StatusCode.ClientErrorNotFound);
  }
  const note = notes[0];
  return {
    id: note._id.toHexString(),
    content: note.content
  };
}
```

Do not forget to add the `userId` in the query. Otherwise, a hacker could find notes of a different user without knowing his/her password.

The insert, update, and remove functions can be implemented as follows. In insert, we set _id to undefined, as MongoDB will add a unique ID itself:

```
export async function insert(request: ServerRequest, session:   Session):
Promise<ItemResult> {
  const user = await getUserOrError(session);
  const content = validate.expect(
    request.query["content"], validate.isString);
  const note: Note = {
    _id: undefined,
    userId: user._id,
    content
  };
  await database.insert(database.notes, note);
  return {
    id: note._id.toHexString(),
    content: note.content
  };
}
export async function update(request: ServerRequest, session:   Session):
Promise<ItemResult> {
  const user = await getUserOrError(session);
  const id = validate.expect(
    request.query["id"], validate.isString);
  const content = validate.expect(
    request.query["content"], validate.isString);
  const note: Note = {
    _id: new ObjectID(id),
    userId: user._id,
    content
  };
  await database.update(database.notes,
    { _id: new ObjectID(id), userId: user._id }, note);
  return {
    id: note._id.toHexString(),
    content: note.content
  };
}
export async function remove(request: ServerRequest, session:   Session) {
  const user = await getUserOrError(session);
  const id = validate.expect(
    request.query["id"], validate.isString);
  await database.remove(database.notes,
    { _id: new ObjectID(id), userId: user._id });
  return {};
}
```

Request handling

In `lib/server/index.ts`, we must add references to these functions in `handleRequest`:

```
async function handleRequest(request: ServerRequest, session: Session):
Promise<ServerResponse | Object> {
  const path = request.path.toLowerCase();

  if (path === "/api/login")
return login(request, session);
  if (path === "/api/logout")
return logout(request, session);
  if (path === "/api/note/list")
return note.list(request, session);
  if (path === "/api/note/insert")
return note.insert(request, session);
  if (path === "/api/note/update")
return note.update(request, session);
  if (path === "/api/note/remove")
return note.remove(request, session);
  if (path === "/api/note/find")
return note.find(request, session);
    throw new ServerError(StatusCode.ClientErrorNotFound);
  }
```

Writing the client side

Just like the weather widget, we will write the client side of the note application with Angular 2. When the application starts, it will try to download the list of notes. If the user is not logged in, we will get an `Unauthorized` error (status code `401`) and show the login form. Otherwise, we can show the menu with all notes, a logout button, and a button to create a new note. When clicking on a note, that note is downloaded and the user can edit it in the note editor. If the user clicks on the **new** button, the user can write the new note in the (same) note editor.

The server uses a cookie to manage the session, so we do not have to do that manually on the client side.

We start with almost the same HTML file saved as `static/index.html`:

```
<!DOCTYPE HTML>
<html>
  <head>
    <title>My Notes</title>
```

```html
    <link rel="stylesheet" href="style.css" />
  </head>
  <body>
    <div id="wrapper">
      <note-application>Loading..</note-application>
      </div>
       <script type="text/javascript">
       var global = window;
      </script>
      <script src="scripts/scripts.js"
type="text/javascript"></script>
  </body>
</html>
```

In `static/style.css`, we add some styles as follows:

```css
body {
    font-family: 'Segoe UI', Tahoma, Geneva, Verdana, sans-serif;
    font-weight: 100;
}
h1, h2, h3 {
  margin: 0 0;
  padding: 0 0;
  color: #C93524;
}
h2 {
  margin: 0 0;
  padding: 0 0;
  color: #1C5C91;
}
#wrapper {
  position: absolute;
  left: 0;
  right: 0;
  top: 0;
  width: 450px;
  margin: 10% auto;
}
a:link, a:visited {
  color: #1C5C91;
  text-decoration: underline;
}
a:hover, a:active {
  color: #3B6282;
}
li >a:link, li >a:visited {
  color: #C93524;
  text-decoration: underline;
```

```
}
li >a:hover, li >a:active {
  color: #AD4236;
}
label {
  display: block;
}
```

In `lib/client/api.ts`, we create a function, `getUrl`, that will simplify API access. With this function, we can write `getUrl("login", { username: "lorem", password: "ipsum" })` instead of `"login?username=lorem&password=ipsum"`. The function also takes the escaping of characters, such as an ampersand, into account:

```
export const baseUrl = "/api/";
export function getUrl(method: string, query: { [key: string]: string }) {
  let url = baseUrl + method;
  let seperator = "?";
  for (const key of Object.keys(query)) {
    url += seperator + encodeURIComponent(key) + "=" +
encodeURIComponent(query[key]);
    seperator = "&";
  }
  return url;
}
```

Creating the login form

Now we can create the login form, as shown in the following screenshot:

In `lib/client/login.ts`, we create the login form. We start with the imports and the template:

```
import { Component, Output, EventEmitter } from "angular2/core";
import { Http, HTTP_PROVIDERS } from "angular2/http";
import { getUrl } from "./api";
import { LoginResult } from "../shared/api";

@Component({
  selector: "login-form",
  template: `
    <h2>Login</h2>
    <form (submit)="submit($event)">
      <div>{{ message }}</div>
      <label>Username<br /><input [(ngModel)]="username"
/></label>
      <label>Password<br /><input type="password"
[(ngModel)]="password" /></label>
      <button type="submit">Log in< /button>
    </form>
    `,
  viewProviders: [HTTP_PROVIDERS]
})
export class LoginForm {
  username: string;
  password: string;
  message: string;

  constructor(private http: Http) {}
```

Here we will submit the username and password to the server. If the login is successful, we emit the success event. The main component can then hide the login page and show the menu:

```
  submit(e: Event) {
    e.preventDefault();
    this.http.get(getUrl("login", { username: this.username,
password: this.password }))
      .map(response =>response.json())
      .subscribe((response: LoginResult) => {
        if (response.ok) {
          this.success.emit(undefined);
          } else {
            this.message = response.message;
        }
      });
  }
```

```
    @Output()
    success = new EventEmitter();
}
```

Creating a menu

In `lib/client/menu.ts`, we create the menu. In the menu, the user will see his/her notes and can create a new note. The menu will look like the following:

```
My Notes
Log out
    New

    • Shoppinglist
    • Todo
```

This component can emit two different events: create and open. The second has an argument, so we have to add `string` as type argument:

```
import { Component, Input, Output, EventEmitter } from "angular2/core";
import { MenuItem } from "../shared/api";

@Component({
  selector: "notes-menu",
  template: `
    <button type="button" (click)="clickCreate()">New</button>
    <ul>
      <li *ngFor="#item of items">
        <a href="javascript:;" (click)="clickItem(item)">{{
item.title }}</a>
      </li>
    </ul>
    `
})
export class Menu {
  @Input()
  items: MenuItem[];

  @Output()
```

```
  create = new EventEmitter();

  @Output()
  open = new EventEmitter<string>();

  clickCreate() {
    this.create.emit(undefined);
  }
  clickItem(item: MenuItem) {
    this.open.emit(item.id);
  }
}
```

The note editor

The note editor is a simple text area. Above it, we will show the title of the note. With two-way bindings, the title is automatically updated when the content of the text area is changed.

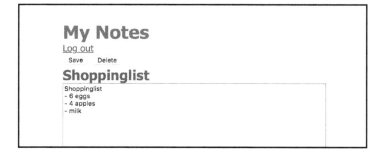

The main component

Now we can write the main component. This component will show one of the other components, depending on the state. First we must import rxjs, Angular, and the functions and components we have already written:

```
import "rxjs";
import { Component } from "angular2/core";
import { bootstrap } from "angular2/platform/browser";
import { Http, HTTP_PROVIDERS, Response } from "angular2/http";
import { getUrl } from "./api";
import { MenuItem, MenuResult, ItemResult } from "../shared/api";
```

```
import { LoginForm } from "./login";
import { Menu } from "./menu";
import { NoteEditor } from "./note";
```

We will use an enum type to store the state:

```
enum State {
  Login,
  Menu,
  Note,
  Error
}
```

The template shows the right component based on the state. These components have some event listeners attached:

```
@Component ({
  selector: "note-application",
  viewProviders: [HTTP_PROVIDERS],
  directives: [LoginForm, Menu, NoteEditor],
  template: `
    <h1>My Notes</h1>
    <login-form *ngIf="stateLogin" (success)="loadMenu()"></login-
form>
      <div *ngIf="!stateLogin">
      <a href="javascript:;" (click)="logout()">Log out</a>
    </div>
    <notes-menu *ngIf="stateMenu" [items]="menu"
(create)="createNote()" (open)="loadNote($event)">        </notes-menu>
    <note-editor *ngIf="stateNote&& note" [content]="note.content"
(save)="save($event)" (remove)="remove($event)"></note-editor>
      <div *ngIf="stateError">
        <h2>Something went wrong</h2>
        Reload the page and try again
      </div>
      `
})
```

In the body of the class, we have to add some properties for the state first:

```
class Application {
  state = State.Menu;

  constructor(private http: Http) {
    this.loadMenu();
  }

  get stateLogin() {
```

```
    return this.state === State.Login;
  }
  get stateMenu() {
    return this.state === State.Menu;
  }
  get stateNote() {
    return this.state === State.Note;
  }
  get stateError() {
    return this.state === State.Error;
  }

  menu: MenuItem[] = [];
  note: ItemResult = undefined;
```

Error handler

Now we will write a function that will load the menu. Errors will be passed to
`handleError`. If the user was not authenticated, we will find the status code `401` here and
show the login form. For a successful request, we can cast the response to the interfaces we
defined in `lib/shared/api.ts`:

```
handleError(error: Response) {
  if (error.status === 401) {
    // Unauthorized
    this.state = State.Login;
    this.menu = [];
    this.note = undefined;
  } else {
    this.state = State.Error;
  }
}
loadMenu() {
    this.state = State.Menu;
    this.menu = [];
    this.http.get(getUrl("note/list", {})).subscribe(response => {
      const body = <MenuResult>response.json();
      this.menu = body.items;
    }, error => this.handleError(error));
  }
```

We implement the event listeners, `createNote` and `loadNote`, of the menu:

```
createNote() {
    this.note = {
      id: undefined,
```

```
      content: ""
    };
    this.state = State.Note;
  }
  loadNote(id: string) {
    this.note = undefined;
    this.http.get(getUrl("note/find", { id: id
  })).subscribe(response => {
      this.state = State.Note;
      this.note = <ItemResult>response.json();
    }, error => this.handleError(error));
  }
```

In `save`, we have to check whether the note is new or being updated:

```
save(content: string) {
    let url: string;
    this.note.content = content;
    if (this.note.id === undefined) {
      // New note
      url = getUrl("note/insert", { content: this.note.content });
    } else {
      // Existing note
      url = getUrl("note/update", { id: this.note.id, content:
this.note.content });
    }

    this.state = State.Note;
    this.note = undefined;
    this.http.get(url).subscribe(response => {
      this.loadMenu();
    }, error => this.handleError(error));
  }
  remove() {
    if (this.note.id === undefined) {
      this.loadMenu();
      return;
    }
    this.http.get(getUrl("note/remove", { id: this.note.id
  })).subscribe(response => {
      this.loadMenu();
    }, error => this.handleError(error));
  }
  logout() {
    this.http.get(getUrl("logout", {})).subscribe(response => {
      this.state = State.Login;
      this.menu = [];
      this.note = undefined;
```

```
    }, error => this.handleError(error));
  }
}

bootstrap(Application).catch(err => console.error(err));
```

Running the application

To test the application, the server and the static files have to be served from the same server. To do that, you can use the `http-server` package. That server can serve the static files and pass through (proxy) the requests to the API server. If MongoDB is not running yet, open a terminal window and run `mongod --dbpath ./data`. Open a terminal window in the root of the project and run the following to start the API server on `localhost:8800`:

gulp && node --harmony_destructuring dist/server

In a new terminal window, navigate to the `static` directory. Install `http-server` using the following command:

npm install http-server -g

Now you can start the server:

http-server -P http://localhost:8800

Open `localhost:8080` in a browser and you will see the application that we have created.

Summary

In this chapter, you created a client-server application. You used NodeJS to create a server, with MongoDB and Phaethon. You also learned more about asynchronous programming and the structural type system. We used our knowledge of Angular from the first chapter to create the client side.

In the next chapter, we will create another client-server application. That application is not a CRUD application, but a real-time chat application. We will be using React instead of Angular.

4
Real-Time Chat

After having written two applications with Angular 2, we will now create one with **React**. The server part will also be different. Instead of a connectionless server, we will now create a server with a persistent connection. In the previous chapters, the client sent requests to the server and the server responded to them. Now we will write a server that can send information at any time to the client. This is needed to send new chat messages immediately to the client, as shown in the following:

In the chat application, a user can first choose a username and join a chat room. In the room, he/she can send messages and receive messages from other users. In this chapter, we will cover the following topics:

- Setting up the project
- Getting started with React
- Writing the server
- Connecting to the server
- Creating the chat room
- Comparing React and Angular

Setting up the project

Before we can start coding, we have to set up the project. The directory structure will be the same as in Chapter 3, *Note-Taking App with Server*; `static` contains the static files for the webserver, `lib/client` contains the client-side code, `lib/server` contains the code for the server, `lib/shared` contains the code that can be used on both sides, and `lib/typings` contains the type definitions for React.

We can install all dependencies, for `gulp`, the server, and React, as follows:

```
npm init
npm install react react-dom ws --save
npm install gulp gulp-sourcemaps gulp-typescript gulp-uglify small --save-
dev
```

The type definitions can be installed using `npm`:

```
cd lib
npm install @types/node @types/react @types/react-dom @types/ws --save
```

We create `static/index.html`, which will load the compiled JavaScript file:

```html
<!DOCTYPE HTML>
<html>
  <head>
    <title>Chat</title>
    <link href="style.css" rel="stylesheet" />
  </head>
  <body>
    <div id="app"></div>
    <script type="text/javascript">
      var process = {
```

```
        env: {
        NODE_ENV: "DEBUG" // or "PRODUCTION"
        }
      };
    </script>
    <script src="scripts/scripts.js" type="text/javascript"></script>
  </body>
</html>
```

We add styles in `static/style.css`:

```
body {
  font-family: 'Segoe UI', Tahoma, Geneva, Verdana, sans-serif;
}
label, input, button {
  display: block;
}
```

Configuring gulp

We can use almost the same `gulpfile`. We do not have to load any polyfills for React, so the resulting file is even simpler:

```
var gulp = require("gulp");
var sourcemaps = require("gulp-sourcemaps");
var typescript = require("gulp-typescript");
var small = require("small").gulp;
var uglify = require("gulp-uglify");

var tsServer = typescript.createProject("lib/tsconfig.json", {
typescript: require("typescript") });

var tsClient = typescript.createProject("lib/tsconfig.json", { typescript:
require("typescript"), target: "es5" });

gulp.task("compile-client", function() {
    return gulp.src(["lib/client/**/*.ts", "lib/client/**/*.tsx",
    "lib/shared/**/*.ts"], { base: "lib" })
        .pipe(sourcemaps.init())
        .pipe(typescript(tsClient))
        .pipe(small("client/index.js", { outputFileName: {
         standalone: "scripts.js" }, externalResolve:
         ["node_modules"] }))
        .pipe(sourcemaps.write("."))
        .pipe(gulp.dest("static/scripts"));
});
```

```
gulp.task("compile-server", function() {
    return gulp.src(["lib/server/**/*.ts", "lib/shared/**/*.ts"], {
    base: "lib" })
        .pipe(sourcemaps.init())
        .pipe(typescript(tsServer))
        .pipe(sourcemaps.write("."))
        .pipe(gulp.dest("dist"));
});
gulp.task("release", ["compile-client", "compile-server"], function() {
    return gulp.src("static/scripts/**.js")
        .pipe(uglify())
        .pipe(gulp.dest("static/scripts"));
});

gulp.task("default", ["compile-client", "compile-server"]);
```

In `lib/tsconfig.json`, we configure TypeScript. We have to set the `jsx` option. In React, views are written in an XML-like language, **JSX**, inside JavaScript. To use this in TypeScript, you have to set the `jsx` option and use the file extension `.tsx` instead of `.jsx`.

```
{
    "compilerOptions": {
        "module": "commonjs",
        "target": "es6",
        "jsx": "react",
        "types": ["node"]
    }
}
```

Getting started with React

Just like Angular, React is component based. Angular is called a framework, whereas React is called a library. This means that Angular provides a lot of different functionalities and React provides one functionality, **views**. In the first two chapters, we used the HTTP service of Angular. React does not provide such a service, but you can use other libraries from npm instead.

Creating a component with JSX

A component is a class that has a render method. That method will render the view and is the replacement of the template in Angular. A simple component would look like the following:

```
export class Example extends React.Component<{}, {}> {
  render() {
    const name = "World";
    return (
      <div>
        Hello, { name }!
        <button onClick={() => alert("Hello")}>
          Click me
          </button>
      </div>
    );
  }
}
```

As you can see, you can embed HTML inside the `render` function. Expressions can be wrapped inside curly brackets, both in text and in properties of other components. Event handlers can be added in this way too. Instead of using built-in components, you can use custom components in these handlers. All built-in components start with a lowercase character and custom elements should start with an uppercase character. This is not just a convention, but required by React. We have to use a different syntax for type casts in `.tsx` files, as the normal syntax conflicts with the XML elements. Instead of `<Type> value`, we will now write `value as Type`. In `.ts` files, we can use both styles.

Adding props and state to a component

In the example, the component extends the `React.Component` class. That class has two type arguments, which represent the props and the state. The props contain the input that the parent component gives to this one. You can compare that to the `@Input` directive in Angular. You cannot modify the props in the containing class. The state contains the other properties of a component in Angular, which can be modified in the class. You can access the props with `this.props` and the state with `this.state`. The state cannot be modified directly, as you have to replace the state with a new object. Imagine the state contains two properties, `foo` and `bar`. If you want to modify `foo` and `bar`, it is not allowed with `this.state.foo = 42`, but you have to write `this.setState({ foo: 42, bar: true })` instead. In most cases, you do not have to change all properties of the state. In such cases, you only have to specify the properties that you want to change. For instance, `this.setState({ foo: 42, bar: true })` will change the value of `foo` and keep the old value of `bar`. The state object is then replaced by a new object. The state object will never change. Such an object is called an immutable object. We will read more on these objects in `Chapter 5`, *Native QR Scanner App*.

The component will be re-rendered by React after calling `setState`.

In other parts of the application, we will also need to modify a few properties of an object. For big objects, this becomes annoying. We create a helper function, which requires the old state, adds modifications to it, and returns a new state. This function does not change the old state, but returns a new one. In `lib/client/model.ts`, we create the `modify` function:

```
export function modify<U extends V, V>(old: U, changes: V) {
  const result: any = Object.create(Object.getPrototypeOf(old));
  for (const key of Object.keys(old)) {
    result[key] = old[key];
  }
  for (const key of Object.keys(changes)) {
    result[key] = changes[key];
  }
  return <U> result;
}
```

Creating the menu

We will start with the menu of our application. In the menu, the user can choose the chat room that he/she wants to join. The menu will first ask the user for a username. Afterward, the user can type the name of a chat room. The user will get completions for known rooms, but he/she can also create a new room. Let's check the following screenshot as an example of menu:

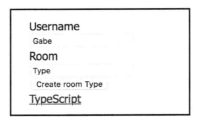

The component will delegate the completions to its parent, so we need to add the current list of completions to the props, such that the parent can set it. Also, we need to add a callback that can be called when the completions must be fetched.

The state must contain the username and the room name. React does not have two-way bindings, so we have to use event listeners to update the username and room name in the state.

We will disable the rest of the menu if the user hasn't provided the username. When the user has filled in a room, we show a list of completions and a button to create a new room with the specified name.

We write the code in `lib/client/menu.tsx`. First, we define the props and state in two different interfaces:

```
import * as React from "react";
import { modify } from "./model";

interface MenuProps {
  completions: string[];
  onRequestCompletions: (room: string) => void;
  onClick: (username: string, room: string) => void;
}
interface MenuState {
  username: string;
  roomname: string;
}
```

Second, we create the class. We set the initial state with an empty username and room name:

```
export class Menu extends React.Component<MenuProps,
MenuState> {
  state = {
    username: "",
    roomname: ""
  };
```

In the render function, we use JSX to show the component. We can use normal TypeScript constructs. There is no need to use something like `NgIf` or `NgFor`, as we did in Angular:

```
render() {
  const menuEnabled = this.state.username !== "";
  const menuStyle = {
    opactity: menuEnabled ? 1 : 0.5
  };
  const showCreateButton = menuEnabled
  && this.state.roomname !== ""
  && this.props.completions
      .indexOf(this.state.roomname) === -1;
  return (<div>
    <label htmlFor="username">Username</label>
    <input type="text" id="username" onChange=
      {e => this.changeUsername(
      (e.target as HTMLInputElement).value)} />
```

```
            <div style={menuStyle}>
              <label htmlFor="roomname">Room</label>
              <input type="text" id="roomname"
                disabled={!menuEnabled}
                 onChange={e =>
                   this.changeName(
                     (e.target as HTMLInputElement).value)
                   } />
              { showCreateButton
                ? <button onClick={
                   () => this.submit(this.state.roomname)}>
                     Create room { this.state.roomname }</button>
              : "" }
              { this.props.completions.map(
                completion =>
                   <a href="javascript:;"
                    key={completion}
                    style={{display: "block"}}
                   onClick={() =>
                   this.submit(completion)}>
                     { completion }</a>) }
            </div>
          </div>);
      }
```

Finally, we can implement the listeners:

```
        private changeUsername(username: string) {
          this.setState({ username });
         }
        private changeName(roomname: string) {
          this.setState({ roomname });
          this.props.onRequestCompletions(roomname);
         }
        private submit(room: string) {
          this.props.onClick(this.state.username, room);
         }
       }
```

We can see this component in action by adding the following in `lib/client/index.tsx`:

```
    ReactDOM.render(<Menu completions={[]} onRequestCompletions={() => {}}
    onClick={() => {}} />);
```

This will render the menu in the HTML file.

Testing the application

To view the application in a browser, you must first build it using `gulp`. You can execute `gulp` in a terminal. Afterward, you can open `static/index.html` in a browser.

Writing the server

To add interaction to the application, we must create the server first. We will use the `ws` package to easily create a websocket server. On the websocket, we can send messages in both directions. These messages are objects converted to strings with JSON, just like in the previous chapters.

Connections

In the previous chapter, we wrote a connectionless server. For every request, a new connection was set up. We could store a state using a session. Such session was identified with a cookie. If you were to copy that cookie to a different computer, you would have the same session there.

Now we will write a server that uses connections. In this way, the server can easily keep track of which user is logged in and where. The server can also send a message to the client without a direct request. This automatic updating is called pushing. The opposite, pulling, or polling, means that the client constantly asks the server whether there is new data.

With connections, the order of arrival is the same as the order of sending. With a connectionless server, a second message can use a different route and arrive earlier.

Typing the API

We will type these messages in `lib/shared/api.ts`. In the previous chapter, the URL identified the function to be called. Now, we must include that information in the message object. We type the messages from the client to the server and vice versa:

```
export enum MessageKind {
    FindRooms,
    OpenRoom,
    SendMessage,

    RoomCompletions,
    ReceiveMessage,
```

```
    RoomContent
}
export interface Message {
  kind: MessageKind;
}

export type ClientMessage = OpenRoom | ChatMessage | FindRooms;
export type ServerMessage = RoomContent | ChatMessage;

export interface FindRooms extends Message {
  query: string;
}
export interface OpenRoom extends Message {
  room: string;
}
export interface RoomCompletions extends Message {
  completions: string[];
}
export interface RoomContent extends Message {
  room: string;
  messages: ChatContent[];
}
export interface SendMessage extends Message {
  text: string;
}
export interface ChatMessage extends Message {
  content: ChatContent
}

export interface ChatContent {
  room: string;
  username: string;
  content: string;
}
```

Accepting connections

In `lib/server/index.ts`, we create a server that listens for new connections. We also keep track of all open connections. When a message is sent in a chat room, it can be forwarded to all sessions that have opened that room. We use `ws` to create a websocket server:

```
import * as WebSocket from "ws";
import * as api from "../shared/api";

const server = new WebSocket.Server({ port: 8800 });
```

```
server.on("connection", receiveConnection);

interface Session {
  sendChatMessage(message: api.ChatContent): void;
}
const sessions: Session[] = [];
```

We will store the recent messages in an array. We limit the size of the array, as an attacker could otherwise fill the whole memory of a server with a (D)DOS attack: if a user sends a lot of messages (automatically), this will cost a lot of server memory. If multiple users do that, the memory can be filled entirely and the server will crash.

Storing recent messages

You can implement this with an array by removing the first message and appending the new message at the end. However, this would shift the whole array, especially large arrays that can take some time. Instead, we use a different approach. We use an array that can be seen as a circle: after the last element comes the first one. We use a variable that points to the oldest message. When a new message is added, the item at the position of the pointer is overwritten with the new message. The pointer is incremented with one and points again to the oldest message. When the messages A, B, C and D are sent with an array size of 3, this can be visualized like the following:

```
[-, -, -]; pointer = 0
[A, -, -]; pointer = 1
[A, B, -]; pointer = 2
[A, B, C]; pointer = 0
[D, B, C]; pointer = 1
```

If you are familiar with analyzing algorithms and **Big-Oh** notation, this takes O(1), whereas the naive idea takes O(n). We create the array in lib/server/index.ts:

```
const recentMessages: api.ChatContent[] = new Array(2048);
let recentMessagesPointer = 0;
```

We do not save the messages to disk. You could do that and use a cache with such array to increase the performance of the server.

Handling a session

For each connection, we have to keep track of the username and room name of the user. We can do that with variables inside the `receiveConnection` function:

```
function receiveConnection(ws: WebSocket) {
  let username: string;
  let room: string;
```

We can listen to the `message` and `close` events. The first is emitted when the client has sent a message in the websocket. The second is emitted when the websocket has been closed. When the socket is closed, we must not send any messages to it and we must remove it from the `sessions` array:

```
ws.on("message", message);
  ws.on("close", close);
  const session: Session = { sendChatMessage };
  sessions.push(session);

  function message(data) {
    try {
      const object = <api.ClientMessage> JSON.parse(data);
      if (typeof object.kind !== "number") return;
      switch (object.kind) {
        case api.MessageKind.FindRooms:
          findRooms(<api.FindRooms> object);
        case api.MessageKind.OpenRoom:
          openRoom(<api.OpenRoom> object);
            break;
            case api.MessageKind.SendMessage:
            chatMessage(<api.SendMessage> object);
                break;
      }
    } catch (e) {
      console.error(e);
    }
  }
  function close() {
    const index = sessions.indexOf(session);
    sessions.splice(index, 1);
  }
  function send(data: api.ServerMessage) {
    ws.send(JSON.stringify(data));
  }
```

The server should always validate the input that it gets. The data could not be a JSON string, which would cause `JSON.parse` to throw an error. `object.kind` might not be a number, as TypeScript does not do any runtime checks. We can validate that with a `typeof` check.

> If you would not have added a `try/catch`, the server would crash if the client sends a message that is not the correct JSON. To prevent this, we will catch that error. For debugging, we write the error on the console.

Implementing a chat message session

Now we can implement the functions that are called when a message comes in. We start with the function that sends a chat message to all active connections in that room and stores it in the array with recent messages:

```
function sendChatMessage(content: api.ChatContent) {
  if (content.room === room) {
    send({
      kind: api.MessageKind.ReceiveMessage,
      content
    });
  }
}

function chatMessage(message: api.SendMessage) {
  if (typeof message.content !== "string") return;

  const content: api.ChatContent = {
    room,
    username,
    content: message.content
  };

  recentMessages[recentMessagesPointer] = content;
  recentMessagesPointer++;
  if (recentMessagesPointer >= recentMessages.length) {
    recentMessagesPointer = 0;
  }

  for (const item of sessions) {
    if (session !== item) item.sendChatMessage(content);
  }
}
```

This will send a chat message to all other sessions in the same room. We insert the message at the right location in `recentMessages` and adjust the pointer.

Finally, we will write the function that gives completions for room names. We do not have an array of room names, so we have to get that information from the recent messages. The resulting array can contain duplicates, so we have to remove these. A naive approach would be to check for every element if it has occurred before in the array. However, this is a slow operation. Instead, we sort the array first. After sorting, we only have to compare each element with the element before it. If these are equal, the second is a duplicate, otherwise it is not. For those familiar with **Big-Oh**, the first approach costs `O(n^2)` and the second one costs `O(n log(n))`. This results in the following function:

```
function findRooms(message: api.FindRooms) {
  const query = message.query;
  if (typeof query !== "string") return;

  const rooms = recentMessages
    .map(msg => msg.room)
    .filter(room => room.toLowerCase().indexOf(query.toLowerCase()) !==
-1)
    .sort();
  const completions: string[] = [];
  let previous: string = undefined;
  for (let room of rooms) {
    if (previous !== room) {
      completions.push(room);
      previous = room;
    }
  }
  send({
  kind: api.MessageKind.RoomCompletions,
  completions
  });
  }
}
```

We have completed the server and can focus on the client side again.

Connecting to the server

We can connect to the server with the `WebSocket` class:

```
const socket = new WebSocket("ws://localhost:8800/");
```

Since we're using React, we add the following to the state. We create a new component, App, that will show the menu or a chat room based on the state. In `lib/client/index.tsx`, we first define the state and props of that component:

```
import * as React from "react";
import * as ReactDOM from "react-dom";
import * as api from "../shared/api";
import * as model from "./model";
import { Menu } from "./menu";
import { Room } from "./room";

interface Props {
  apiUrl: string;
}
interface State {
  socket: WebSocket;
  username: string;
  connected: boolean;
  completions: string[];
  room: model.Room;
}
class App extends React.Component<Props, State> {
  state = {
    socket: undefined,
    username: '',
    connected: false,
    completions: [],
    room: undefined
  };
```

Automatic reconnecting

Next up, we will write a function, `connect`, that connects to the server using a `WebSocket`. We call that function in `componentDidMount`, which is called by React. We must also call `connect` when the connection gets closed for some reason (for instance, network problems). We store the socket in the state and we also keep track of whether the client is connected:

```
connect() {
if (this.state.connected) return;
```

```
const socket = new WebSocket(this.props.apiUrl);
this.setState({ socket });
socket.onopen = () => {
this.setState({ connected: true });
if (this.state.room) {
this.openRoom(this.state.username, this.state.room.name);
}
};
socket.onmessage = e => this.onMessage(e);
socket.onclose = e => {
this.setState({ connected: false });
setTimeout(() => this.connect(), 400);
};
}
onMessage(e: MessageEvent) {
const message = JSON.parse(e.data.toString()) as api.ServerMessage;
if (message.kind === api.MessageKind.RoomCompletions) {
this.setState({
completions: (message as api.RoomCompletions).completions
});
} else if (message.kind === api.MessageKind.RoomContent) {
this.setState({
room: {
name: (message as api.RoomContent).room,
messages: (message as api.RoomContent).messages.map(msg =>
this.mapMessage(msg))
}
});
} else if (message.kind === api.MessageKind.ReceiveMessage) {
this.addMessage(this.mapMessage((message as api.ReceiveMessage).content));
}
}
componentDidMount() {
this.connect();
}
```

`socket.onmessage` is called when the client receives a message from the server. Based on the `kind` of message, it is sent to some function that we will implement later. First, we will write the render function. After we have written the render function, we know which event handlers we have to write.

 When you write **top down**, you first write the main function and afterward the helper functions that the main function requires. With the **bottom up** approach, you write the helper functions before you write the main function. In this section, we write the helper functions last, so we write top down. You can try both styles and find out what you like most.

In `render`, we render the component based on the state—if there is no connection, we show **Connecting...**, if the user is in a room, we show that chat room, otherwise we show the menu:

```
render() {
    if (!this.state.connected) {
        return <div>Connecting...</div>;
    }
    if (this.state.room) {
        return <Room room={this.state.room} onPost={content =>
this.post(content)} />;
    }
    return <Menu
        completions={this.state.completions}
        onRequestCompletions={query =>
this.requestCompletions(query)}
        onClick={(username, room) =>
this.openRoom(username, room)}
    />;
}
```

Sending a message to the server

Before writing the event handlers, we first write a small function that sends a message to the server. It converts an object to JSON, and TypeScript will check that we are sending a correct message to the server:

```
private send(message: api.ClientMessage) {
    this.state.socket.send(JSON.stringify(message));
}
```

The `requestCompletions` and `openRoom` functions send a message to the server. In `openRoom`, we also have to store the username in the state:

```
private requestCompletions(query: string) {
    this.send({
        kind: api.MessageKind.FindRooms,
        query
    });
}
private openRoom(username, room: string) {
    this.send({
        kind: api.MessageKind.OpenRoom,
        username,
        room
    });
```

```
    this.setState({ username });
  }
```

Writing the event handler

For iterations in React, every element should have a key that can identify it. Thus, we need to give every message such a key. We use a simple numeric key, which we will increment for every message:

```
private nextMessageId: number = 0;
private post(content: string) {
  this.send({
    kind: api.MessageKind.SendMessage,
    content
  });
  this.addMessage({
    id: this.nextMessageId++,
    user: this.state.username,
    content,
    isAuthor: true
  });
}
private addMessage(msg: model.Message) {
  const messages = [
    ...this.state.room.messages,
    msg
  ].slice(Math.max(0, this.state.room.messages.length - 10));
  const room = model.modify(this.state.room, {
    messages
  });
  this.setState({ room });
}
private mapMessage(msg: api.ChatContent) {
  return {
    id: this.nextMessageId++,
    user: msg.username,
    content: msg.content,
    isAuthor: msg.username === this.state.username
  };
}
}
```

Finally, we can show the component in the HTML file:

```
ReactDOM.render(
<App apiUrl="ws://localhost:8800/" />, document.getElementById("app")
);
```

We have now written all event handlers and interaction with the server. We write the chat room component in the next section.

Creating the chat room

We divide the chat room into two subcomponents: a message and the input box. When the user sends a new message, it is sent to the main component. Message of the user will be shown on the right and other messages on the left, as shown in the following screenshot:

Two-way bindings

React does not have two-way bindings. Instead, we can store the value in the state and modify it when the onChange event is fired. For the input box, we will use this technique. The textbox should be emptied when the user has sent his/her message. With this binding, we can easily do that by modifying the value in the state to an empty string:

```
class InputBox extends React.Component<{ onSubmit(value: string): void; },
{ value: string }> {
  state = {
```

```
      value: ""
    };
    render() {
      return (
        <form onSubmit={e => this.submit(e)}>
        <input onChange={e => this.changeValue((e.target as
HTMLInputElement).value)} value={this.state.value} />
          <button disabled={this.state.value === ""}
type="submit">Submit</button>
        </form>
      );
    }
    private changeValue(value: string) {
      this.setState({ value });
    }
    private submit(e: React.FormEvent<{}>) {
      e.preventDefault();
      if (this.state.value) {
        this.props.onSubmit(this.state.value);
        this.state.value = "";
      }
    }
  }
}
```

Stateless functional components

If a component doesn't need a state, then it does not need a class to store and manage that state. Instead of writing a class with just a render function, you can write that function without the class. These components are called stateless functional components. A message is clearly stateless, as you cannot modify a message that has already been sent:

```
function Message(props: { message: model.Message }) {
  return (
    <div>
      <div className={props.message.isAuthor ? "message          message-
own" : "message"}>
        { props.message.content }
        <div className="message-user">
        { props.message.user }
        </div>
      </div>
      <div style={{clear: "both"}}></div>
    </div>
  );
}
```

A stateless functional component can have a child component with a state. The input box has a state and can be used inside Room, which is a stateless component. We have to set the key property in the array of messages. React uses this to identify components inside the array:

```
export function Room(props: { room: model.Room, onPost: (content: string)
=> void }) {
  return (
    <div>
      <h2>{props.room.name}</h2>
      {props.room.messages.map(message => <Message
key={message.id} message={message} />)}
      <Input onSubmit={content => props.onPost(content)} />
    </div>
  );
}
```

Running the application

We can now run the whole application. First, we must compile it with gulp. Second, we can start the server by running `node dist/server` in a terminal. Finally, we can open `static/index.html` in a browser and start chatting. When you open this page multiple times, you can simulate multiple users.

Comparing React and Angular

In the previous chapters, we used Angular and in this chapter we used React. Angular and React are both focused on components, but there are differences, for instance, between the templates in Angular and the views in React. In this section, you can read more about these differences.

Templates and JSX

Angular uses a template for the view of a component. Such a template is a string that is parsed at runtime. TypeScript cannot check these templates. If you misspell a property name, you will not get a compile error.

React uses JSX, which is syntactic sugar around function calls. A JSX element is transformed, by the compiler, into a call to `React.createElement`. The first argument is the name of the element or the element class, the second argument contains the props, and the other arguments are the children of the component. The following example demonstrates the transform:

```
<div></div>;
React.createElement("div", null);

<div prop="a"></div>;
React.createElement("div", { prop: "a" });

<div>Foo</div>;
React.createElement(
    "div",
    null,
    "Foo"
);

<div><span>Foo</span></div>;
React.createElement(
    "div",
    null,
    React.createElement(
        "span",
        null,
        "Foo"
    )
);
```

Elements that start with a capital letter or contain a dot are considered to be custom components, and other elements are treated as intrinsic elements, the standard HTML elements:

```
<div></div>;
React.createElement("div", null);

<Foo></Foo>;
React.createElement(Foo, null);
```

These JSX elements are checked and transformed at compile time, so you do get an early error when you misspell a property. React is not the only framework that uses JSX, but it is the most popular one.

Libraries or frameworks

Angular is a framework and React is a library. A library provides one functionality in the case of React—the views of the application. A framework provides a lot of different functionalities. For instance, Angular renders the views of the application, but also has, for instance, dependency injection and an `Http` service. If you want such features when you are using React, you can use another library that gives that feature.

React programmers often use a Flux based architecture. Flux is an application architecture that is implemented in various libraries. In `Chapter 5`, *Native QR Scanner App*, we will take a look at this architecture.

Summary

We have written an application with websockets. We have used React and JSX for the views of our application. We have seen multiple ways to create components and learned how the JSX transform works. In `Chapter 5`, *Native QR Scanner App*, we will use React again, but we will first take a look at mobile apps with NativeScript in the next chapter.

5
Native QR Scanner App

We have already used TypeScript to build web apps and a server. TypeScript can also be used to create mobile apps. In this chapter, we will build such an app. The app can scan QR codes. The app shows a list of all previous scans. If a QR code contains a URL, the app can open that URL in a web browser. Various frameworks exist for making mobile apps in TypeScript. We will use **NativeScript**, which provides a native user interface and runs on Android and iOS, as shown in the following:

We will create this app with the following steps:

- Creating the project structure
- Creating a Hello World page
- Creating the main view
- Adding a details view
- Scanning QR codes
- Adding persistent storage
- Styling the app
- Comparing NativeScript to alternatives

Getting started with NativeScript

Installing NativeScript requires several steps. For developing apps for Android, you have to install **Java Development Kit (JDK)** and the **Android SDK**. Android apps can be built on Windows, Linux, and Mac. Apps for iOS can only be built on a Mac. You need to install **XCode** to build these apps.

You can find more details on how to install the Android SDK at `https://docs.nativesc ript.org/start/quick-setup`.

After installing the Android SDK or XCode, you can install NativeScript using npm:

```
npm install nativescript -g
```

You can see whether your system is configured correctly by running the following command:

```
tns doctor
```

If you only want to develop apps for iOS, you can ignore the errors on Android and vice versa.

We can test most parts of the app in a simulator that is included in the **SDK** or **XCode**. Scanning a QR code only works on a device.

 Setting up XCode for iOS development is easier than installing the Android SDK. If you can choose between iOS and Android, you want to choose iOS.

Creating the project structure

In the previous chapters, we wrote our TypeScript sources in the `lib` directory. The `static` or `dist` directory contained the compiled sources. However, in this chapter, we have to make a different structure since NativeScript has some requirements on it. NativeScript requires that the compiled sources are located in the `app` directory and it uses the `lib` directory for plugins, so we cannot use that directory for our TypeScript sources. Instead, we will use the `src` directory.

NativeScript can automatically create a basic project structure. By running the following commands, a minimal project will be created:

```
tns init
npm install
```

The first command creates the `package.json` file and the `app` directory. NativeScript stores the icons and splash screens (which you see when the app is loading) in `app`. You can edit these files when you want to publish an app. The `npm install` command installs the dependencies that NativeScript needs. These dependencies were added to `package.json` by the first command.

We need to make some adjustments to it. We must create an `app/package.json` file. NativeScript uses this file to get the main file of the project:

```
{
    "main": "app.js"
}
```

Adding TypeScript

By default, NativeScript apps should be written in JavaScript. We will not use `gulp` to compile our TypeScript files since NativeScript has built-in support for transpilers like TypeScript. We can add TypeScript to it by running the following command:

```
tns install typescript
```

After running this command, NativeScript will automatically compile TypeScript to JavaScript. This command has created two files: `tsconfig.json` and `references.d.ts`. The `tsconfig` file contains the configuration for TypeScript. We will add the `outDir` option to `tsconfig.json` so that we do not have to place the source files in the same direction as the compiled files. NativeScript requires that JavaScript files are placed in the app folder. We will write our TypeScript sources in the `src` folder, and the compiler will write the output to the app folder:

```json
{
    "compilerOptions": {
        "module": "commonjs",
        "target": "es5",
        "inlineSourceMap": true,
        "experimentalDecorators": true,
        "noEmitHelpers": true,
        "outDir": "app"
    },
    "exclude": [
        "node_modules",
        "platforms"
    ]
}
```

The `references.d.ts` file contains a reference to the definition files (`.d.ts` files) of the core modules of NativeScript.

Creating a Hello World page

To get started with NativeScript, we will first write a simple app. In `src/app.ts`, we must register `mainEntry` that will create the view of the app. The entry should be a function that returns a `Page`. A `Page` attribute is one of the classes that NativeScript uses for the user interface. We can create a basic page as follows:

```
import * as application from "application";
import { Page } from "ui/page";
import { Label } from "ui/label";

application.mainEntry = () => {
  const page = new Page();
  const label = new Label();
  label.text = "Hello, World";
  page.content = label;
  return page;
};
application.start();
```

This will create a single label and add it to the page. The content of the page should be a `View` class, which is the base class that all components (including `Label`) in NativeScript inherit.

You can run the app with one of the following commands for Android and iOS, respectively:

```
tns run android --emulator
tns run ios --emulator
```

You can run the app on a device by removing `--emulator`. Your device should be connected using a USB cable. You can see all connected devices by running `tns device`.

NativeScript prints a lot on the console after the output of TypeScript. Make sure you do not miss any compile errors of TypeScript.

On iOS, the app will now look like the following:

In the next sections, we will see how we can add event listeners and build bigger views.

Creating the main view

The main view will show a list of recent scans. Clicking on one of the recent scans opens a details page that shows more details on the scan. When a user clicks on the **Scan** button, the user can scan a QR code using the camera:

First, we create the model of a scan in `src/model.ts`. We need to store the content (a string) and the date of the scan:

```
export interface Scan {
  content: string;
  date: Date;
}
```

In `src/view/main.ts`, we will create the view. The view should export a function that creates the page, so we can use it as the `mainEntry`. It also needs to export a function that can update the content. The view has two callbacks or events: one is called when an item is clicked and the other is called when the user clicks on the **Scan** button. This can be implemented by adding the two callbacks as arguments of the `createPage` function and returning `setItems`, which updates the content of the list, and `createView`, which creates the `Page`, as an object:

```
import { Page } from "ui/page";
import { ActionBar, ActionItem } from "ui/action-bar";
import { ListView } from "ui/list-view";

export function createPage(itemCallback: (index: number) => void,
scanCallback: () => void) {
  let items: string[] = [];
  let list: ListView;

  return { setItems, createView };
  function setItems(value: string[]) {
    items = value;
    if (list) {
      list.items = items;
      list.refresh();
    }
  }
}
```

An `ActionBar` is the bar at the top of the screen with the app name. We add an `ActionItem` attribute to it, which is a button in the bar. We use a `ListView` attribute to show the recent scans in a list. Elements have an `on` method, which we use to listen to events, similar to `addEventListener` in websites and `on` in NodeJS.

The `itemLoading` event is fired when an item in the list is being rendered. In that event, the view for an item of the list should be created. The `tap` event is fired when the user taps on the scan button. The `itemCallback` event will be invoked with the index of the item when that happens.

First, we create the action bar. We add it to the page and add a button to the action bar:

```
function createView() {
  const page = new Page();
  const actionBar = new ActionBar();
  actionBar.title = "QR Scanner";
  const buttonScan = new ActionItem();
  buttonScan.text = "Scan";
  buttonScan.on("tap", scanCallback);
  actionBar.actionItems.addItem(buttonScan);
```

Next, we create the list as follows:

```
list = new ListView();
list.items = items;
```

Finally, we add event listeners to the list. In `itemLoading`, we create `Label`, if it was not created yet, and set the text of it. In `itemTap`, we call `itemCallback` with the index of the tapped item:

```
list.on("itemLoading", args => {
  if (!args.view) {
    args.view = new Label();
  }
  (<Label> args.view).text = items[args.index];
});
list.on("itemTap", e => itemCallback(e.index));

page.actionBar = actionBar;
page.content = list;
return page;
  }
}
```

In `src/app.ts`, we can call this function and show the `view` attribute:

```
import * as application from "application";
import { createPage } from "./view/main";
import * as model from "./model";

let items: model.Scan[] = [];

const page = createPage(index => showDetailsPage(items[index]), scan);
application.mainEntry = page.createView;
application.cssFile = "style.css";
application.start();
```

We will implement scanning later on. For now, we will always add a fake scan, so we can test the other parts of the application:

```
function scan() {
    addItem("Lorem");
}
```

In `addItem`, we add a new scan to the list of scans. We call `update`, which will update the list in the main view and show the details page with this scan. We limit the amount of scans in the list by `100`:

```
function addItem(content: string) {
    const item: model.Scan = {
        content,
        date: new Date()
    };
    items = [item, ...items].slice(0, 100);
    update();
    showDetailsPage(item);
}
```

We will implement the details page in the next section. For now, we will only add a placeholder function so that we can test the other functions:

```
function showDetailsPage(scan: model.Scan) {
}
```

In `update`, we change the values in the list to the new items:

```
function update() {
    page.setItems(items.map(item => item.content));
}
```

Adding a details view

The details view is shown when the user scans a code or clicks on an item in the recent scans list. It shows the content of the scan and the date, as shown in the following screenshot:

If the content of the scan is a URL, we will show a button to open that link, as shown in the following screenshot:

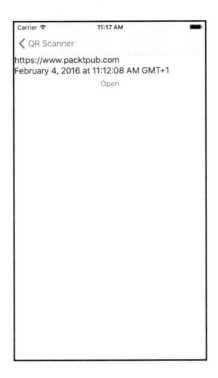

At the end of this chapter, we will style this page properly.

We add a function to `src/model.ts` that will return `true` when the scan (probably) contains a URL. We consider a scan that contains no spaces and begins with `http://` or `https://` to be a URL:

```
function startsWith(input: string, start: string) {
  return input.substring(0, start.length) === start;
}
export function isUrl({ content }: Scan) {
  if (content.indexOf(" ") !== -1) {
    return false;
  }
  return startsWith(content, "http://") || startsWith(content,
"https://");
}
```

The view requires the scan itself and optionally a callback. The callback will only be provided if the scan contains a link and the button should be shown.

NativeScript has various ways to show multiple elements on a page. A page can only contain a single component, but NativeScript has components that can contain multiple components. These are called layouts. The simplest one, and probably also the most used, is the StackLayout. Elements will be placed below or beside each other. The StackLayout has a property orientation that indicates whether the elements should be placed below (vertical, default) or beside (horizontal) each other.

Other layouts include the following:

- **DockLayout**: Elements can be placed on the left, right, top, bottom, or center of the component.
- **GridLayout**: Elements are placed in one or multiple rows and columns in a grid. This is equal to a <table> tag in HTML.
- **WrapLayout**: A row is filled with elements. When it is full, the next elements are added to a new row.

You can find all components at http://docs.nativescript.org/ui/ui-views and all layout containers at http://docs.nativescript.org/ui/layout-containers.

In src/view/details.ts, we will implement this page:

```
import { EventData } from "data/observable";
import { topmost } from "ui/frame";
import { Page } from "ui/page";
import { ActionBar, ActionItem } from "ui/action-bar";
import { Button } from "ui/button";
import { Label } from "ui/label";
import { StackLayout } from "ui/layouts/stack-layout";
import * as model from "../model";

export function createDetailsPage(scan: model.Scan, callback?: () => void)
{
  return { createView };
  function createView() {
    const page = new Page();
    const layout = new StackLayout();
    page.content = layout;
```

In a label, we will show the content of the scan. We can add a class name to it, just like you would do on an HTML webpage. Later on, we can style this page using CSS:

```
const label = new Label();
label.text = scan.content;
label.className = "details-content";
layout.addChild(label);
```

The date of the scan will be shown in a second label:

```
const date = new Label();
date.text = scan.date.toLocaleString("en");
layout.addChild(date);
```

If a callback is provided, we show a button that will open the link of the scan:

```
if (callback) {
  const button = new Button();
  button.text = "Open";
  button.on("tap", callback);
  layout.addChild(button);
}

return page;
  }
}
```

In `src/app.ts`, we can now implement the `showDetailsPage` function. Using `topmost().navigate`, we can navigate to the page. Users can go back to the main page with the standard back button of Android or iOS, which is automatically shown:

```
import { topmost } from "ui/frame";
import { openUrl } from "utils/utils";
import { createDetailsPage } from "./view/details";
...
function showDetailsPage(scan: model.Scan) {
  let callback: () => void;
  if (model.isUrl(scan)) {
    callback = () => openUrl(scan.content);
  }
  topmost().navigate(createDetailsPage(scan, callback).createView);
}
```

The `openUrl` function opens a web browser with the specified URL.

Scanning QR codes

NativeScript has support for plugins. A plugin can add extra functionality, such as turning on the flash light of a phone, vibrating the phone, logging in with Facebook, or scanning QR codes. These can be installed using the command line interface of NativeScript.

We will use a NativeScript plugin to scan QR codes. The plugin is called NativeScript BarcodeScanner. It can scan QR codes and other barcode formats. The plugin can be installed using the following command:

```
tns plugin add nativescript-barcodescanner
```

Type definitions

We must add a definition file to import the plugin. The plugin does not contain type definitions, and type definitions are not available on DefinitelyTyped and TSD. It is not necessary to write definitions that are fully correct. We only have to type the parts of the library that we are using. We use the scan function, which can take an optional settings object and return a `Promise`. In `src/definitions.d.ts`, we write the following definition:

```
declare module "nativescript-barcodescanner" {
    function scan(options?: any): Promise<any>;
}
```

 You do not need to specify the `export` keyword in definition files. All declarations in a module in a definition file are automatically considered to be exported.

Implementation

The `scan` function can now be implemented. We use the exported `scan` function and listen for `Promise` to resolve or reject. When `Promise` resolves, we add the item to the list and open the details page.

We can import the plugin in `src/app.ts`:

```
import * as barcodescanner from "nativescript-barcodescanner";
```

The `scan` function can now be rewritten as follows:

```
function scan() {
  barcodescanner.scan().then(result => {
    addItem(result.text);
    return false;
  });
}
```

We can also show a message when the scan failed. This way, the user gets feedback when the scan failed. We will show a question asking whether the user wants to try again, as shown in the following screenshot:

This can be implemented by replacing the `scan` function with the following code:

```
import * as dialogs from "ui/dialogs";
...
function scan() {
  barcodescanner.scan().then(result => {
    addItem(result.text);
    return false;
```

```
  }, () => {
    return dialogs.confirm("Failed to scan a barcode. Try again?")
  }).then(tryAgain => {
    if (tryAgain) {
      scan();
    }
  });
}
```

In the first callback, the scan was successful. The scan is added to the recent scan list and the details page shows. In the second callback, we show the dialog. The `dialogs.confirm` function returns a promise, which will resolve to `boolean`. In the last callback, `tryAgain` will be `false` if the scan was successful or if the user clicked on the **No** button. It will be true if the user clicked on the **Yes** button. In that case, we will show the barcode scanner again.

> When you return a value in the second callback (or `catch` callback), the resulting `Promise` will resolve to that value. When you return `Promise`, the resulting `Promise` will be resolved or rejected with the value or error of that `Promise`. If you want to reject the resulting `Promise`, you must use `throw`.

Testing on a device

In the emulator, we cannot take a picture of a QR code; thus, we have to test the app on a device. We can do that by connecting the device using a USB cable and then running `tns run android` or `tns run ios`. You can test the app using these QR codes, which contain text (left image) and a URL (right image). You can scan the QR codes several times and notice the list build up in the main view. When you restart the app, you will see that the list is cleared. We will fix that in the next section.

Adding persistent storage

When the user closes and reopens the app, the user sees an empty list of scans. We can make the list persistent by saving it after a scan and loading it when the app starts. We can use the `application-settings` module to store the scans. The storage is based on **key-value**: a value is assigned to a specific key.

Only booleans, numbers, and strings can be stored using this module. An array cannot be stored. Instead, one could store the length under one key (for instance, `items-length`) and the items under a set of keys (`items-0`, `items-1`, ...). An easier approach is to convert the array to a string using **JSON**.

The list can be saved using the following function:

```
function save() {
  applicationSettings.setString("items", JSON.stringify(items));
}
```

The `Date` objects are converted to strings by `JSON.stringify`. Thus, we must convert them back to a `Date` object manually:

```
function load() {
  const data = applicationSettings.getString("items");
  if (data) {
    try {
      items = (<any[]> JSON.parse(data)).map(item => ({
        content: item.content,
        date: new Date(item.date)
      }));
    } catch (e) {}
  }
}
```

Before `application.start()`, we must call the `load` and `update` functions to show the previous scans:

```
const page = createPage(index => showDetailsPage(items[index]), scan);
application.mainEntry = page.createView;
load();
update();
application.start();
```

In `addItem`, we must call `save`:

```
function addItem(content: string) {
  const item: model.Scan = {
    content,
    date: new Date()
  };
  items = [item, ...items].slice(0, 100);
  save();
  update();
  showDetailsPage(item);
}
```

Styling the app

The app can be styled using CSS. Not all CSS properties are supported, but basic settings like fonts, colors, margin, and padding work. We can add a stylesheet in the app adding the following code before `application.start()`:

```
application.cssFile = "style.css";
```

We will change the style of the following parts of the app:

In `app/style.css`, we will first give the `ActionBar` a background color:

```
ActionBar {
  background-color: #237691;
  color: #fefefe;
}
```

 The stylesheet must be added in the `app` folder, instead of `src`. NativeScript will only load files inside `app`. TypeScript files are compiled into that folder, but the stylesheet should already be located there.

We will add some margin to the labels in the list and details page:

```
Label {
  margin: 10px;
}
```

The main page is now properly styled, as shown in the following screenshot:

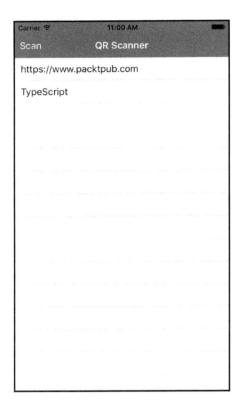

We can also style the label on the **detail** page, which we gave a class name. We make the text in the label bigger and center the text:

```
.details-content {
  font-size: 28pt;
  text-align: center;
  margin: 10px;
}
```

This results in the following design:

Comparing NativeScript to alternatives

Various frameworks that can build mobile apps exist. Lots of developers use **Cordova** or **Phonegap**. These tools wrap an HTML page into an app. These apps are called hybrid, as they combine HTML pages with mobile apps. The user interface is not native and can give a bad user experience.

Other tools have a native interface, which gives a good look and feel. **Titanium**, **NativeScript**, and **React Native** do this. With these tools, less code can be shared between a web app and mobile app. With React Native, apps can be written using the React framework.

In NativeScript, programmers have access to all native APIs. The disadvantage of this is that the programmer would write platform-specific code. NativeScript also includes wrappers around these classes, which work on both Android and iOS. For instance, the `Button` class, which we used in this chapter, is a wrapper around `android.widget.Button` on Android and `UIButton` on iOS.

Summary

In this chapter, we created a mobile app using NativeScript. We used a plugin to scan QR codes. The scans are saved, so the list is persisted after a restart of the app. Finally, we added custom styles to our app.

In the next chapter, we will build a spreadsheet web app using React. We will discover some principles of functional programming and learn how we can handle the state of an application. We will also see how we can build a cross-platform application.

6
Advanced Programming in TypeScript

In the previous chapters, we learned the basics of TypeScript and we worked with various frameworks. We will discover more advanced features of TypeScript in this chapter. This chapter covers the following aspects:

- Using type guards
- More accurate type guards
- Checking null and undefined
- Creating tagged union types
- Comparing performance of algorithms

Using type guards

Sometimes, you must check whether a value is of a certain type. For instance, if you have a value of a class `Base`, you might want to check if it is of a certain subclass `Derived`. In JavaScript you would write this with an `instanceof` check. Since TypeScript is an extension of JavaScript, you can also use `instanceof` in TypeScript. In other typed languages, like C#, you must then add a **type cast**, which tells the compiler that a value is of a type, different from what the compiler analyzed. You can also add type casts in two different ways. The old syntax for type casts uses < and >, the new syntax uses the `as` keyword. You can see them both in the next example:

```
class Base {
  a: string;
}
class Derived extends Base {
```

```
    b: number;
}
const foo: Base;
if (foo instanceof Derived) {
    (<Derived> foo).b;
    (foo as Derived).b;
}
```

When you use a type guard, you say to the compiler: trust me, this value will always be of this type. The compiler cannot check that and will assume that it is true. But, we are using a compiler to get notified about errors so we want to reduce the amount of casts that we need.

Luckily, the compiler can, in most cases, understand the usages of instanceof. Thus, in the previous example the compiler knows that the type of foo is Derived inside the if-block. Thus, we do not need type casts there:

```
const foo: Base;
if (foo instanceof Derived) {
    foo.b;
}
```

An expression that checks whether a value is of a certain type is called a **type guard**. TypeScript supports three different kinds of type guards:

- The typeof guard checks for primitive types. It starts typeof x === or typeof x !==, followed by string, number, boolean, object, function, or symbol.
- The instanceof guard checks for class types. Such a type guard starts with the variable name, followed by instanceof and the class name.
- **User defined type guards** a custom type guard. You can define a custom type guard as a function with a special return type:

  ```
  function isCat(animal: Animal): animal is Cat {
      return animal.name === "Kitty";
  }
  ```

You can then use it as isCat(x).

You can use these type guards in the condition of if, while, for, and do-while statements and in the first operand of binary logical operators (x && y, x || y) and conditional expressions (x ? y : z).

Narrowing

The type of a variable will change (locally) after a type guard. This is called **narrowing**. The type will be more specific after narrowing. More specific can mean that a class type is replaced by the type of a subclass, or that a union is replaced by one of its parts. The latter is demonstrated in the following example:

```
let x: string | number;
if (typeof x === "string") {
  // x: string
} else {
  // x: number
}
```

As you can see, a type guard can also narrow a variable in the `else` block.

Narrowing any

Narrowing will give a more specific type. For instance, `string` is more specific than `any`. The following code will narrow x from `any` to `string`:

```
let x: any;
if (typeof x === "string") {
  // x: string
}
```

In general, a more specific type can be used on more constructs than the initial type. For instance, you can call `.substring` on a string, but not on a `string | number`. When narrowing from any, that is not the case. You may write `x.abcd` if x has the type `any`, but not when its type is `string`. In this case, a more specific type allows less constructs with that value. To prevent these issues, the compiler will only narrow values of type `any` to primitive types. That means that a value can be narrowed to `string`, but not to a class type, for instance. The next example demonstrates a case where the compiler would give an undesired error, if this was not implemented:

```
let x: any;
if (x instanceof Object) {
  x.abcd();
}
```

In the block after the type guard, x should not be narrowed to `Object`.

Combining type guards

Type guards can be combined in two ways. First, you can nest if statements and thus apply multiple type guards to a variable:

```
let x: string | number | boolean;
if (typeof x !== "string") {
  if (typeof x !== "number") {
    // x: boolean
  }
}
```

Secondly, you can also combine type guards with the logical operators (&&, ||). The previous example can also be written as:

```
let x: string | number | boolean;
if (typeof x !== "string" && typeof x !== "number") {
  // x: boolean
}
```

With ||, we can check that a value matches one of multiple type guards:

```
let x: string | number | boolean;
if (typeof x === "string" || typeof x === "number") {
  // x: string | number
} else {
  // x: boolean
}
```

More complex type guards can be created with user defined type guards.

More accurate type guards

Before TypeScript 2.0, the compiler did not use the control flow of the program for type guards. The easiest way to see what that means, is by an example:

```
function f(x: string | number) {
  if (typeof x === "string") {
    return;
  }
  x;
}
```

The type guard narrows x to string in the block after the if statement. If the else block existed, it would have narrowed x to number there. Outside of the if statement, no narrowing happens, because the compiler only looks at the structure or shape of the program. That means that the type of x on the last line would be string | number, even though that line can only be executed if the condition of the if statement is false and x can only be a number there. With some terminology, type guards were only syntax directed and were only based on the syntax, not on the control flow of the program.

As of TypeScript 2.0, the compiler can follow the control flow of the program. This gives more accurate types after type guards. The compiler understands that the last line of the function can only be reached if x is not a string. The type of x on the last line will now be number. This analysis is called **control flow based type analysis**.

Assignments

Previously, the compiler did not follow assignments of a variable. If a variable was reassigned in the block after an if statement, the narrowing would not be applied. Thus, in the next example, the type of x is string | number, both before and after the assignment:

```
let x: string | number = ...;
if (typeof x === "string") {
  x = 4;
}
```

With control flow based type analysis, these assignments can be checked. The type of x will be string before the assignment and number after it. Narrowing after an assignment works only for union types. The parts of the union type are filtered based on the assigned value. For types other than union types, the type of the variable will be reset to the initial type after an assignment.

This can be used to write a function that either accepts one value or a list of values, in one of the following ways:

```
function f(x: string | string[]) {
  if (typeof x === "string") x = [x];
  // x: string[]
}
function g(x: string | string[]) {
  if (x instanceof Array) {
    for (const item of x) g(item);
    return;
  }
  // x: string
```

```
}
```

With the same analysis, the compiler can also check for values that are possibly null or undefined. Instead of getting runtime errors saying **undefined is not an object**, you will get a compile time warning that a variable might be undefined or null.

Checking null and undefined

TypeScript 2.0 introduces two new types: `null` and `undefined`. You have to set the compiler option `strictNullChecks` to `true` to use these types. In this mode, all other types cannot contain `undefined` or `null` anymore. If you want to declare a variable that can be `undefined` or `null`, you have to annotate it with a union type. For instance, if you want a variable that should contain a `string` or `undefined`, you can declare it as `let x: string | undefined;`.

Before assignments, the type of the variable will be `undefined`. Assignments and type guards will modify the type locally.

Guard against null and undefined

TypeScript has various ways to check whether a variable could be `undefined` or `null`. The next code block demonstrates them:

```
let x: string | null | undefined = ...;
if (x !== null) {
  // x: string | undefined
}
if (x !== undefined) {
  // x: string | null
}
if (x != null) {
  // x: string
}
if (x) {
  // x: string
}
```

The last type guard can have unexpected behavior, so it is advised to use the others instead. At runtime, x is converted to a Boolean. `null` and `undefined` are both converted to `false`, non-empty strings to `true`, but an empty string is converted to `false`. The latter is not always desired.

To check for a string, you can also use `typeof x === "string"` as a type guard. It is not always possible to write a type guard for some types, but you can always use the type guards in the code block.

The never type

TypeScript 2.0 also introduced the `never` type, which represents an unreachable value. For instance, if you write a function that always throws an error, its return type will be `never`.

```
function alwaysThrows() {
  throw new Error();
}
```

In a union type, `never` will disappear. Formally, `T | never` and `never | T` are equal to `T`. You can use this to create an assertion that a certain position in your code is unreachable:

```
function unreachable() {
  throw new Error("Should be unreachable");
}
function f() {
  switch (...) {
    case ...:
      return true;
    case ...:
      return false;
    default:
      return unreachable();
  }
}
```

The compiler takes the union of the types of all expressions in return statements. That gives `boolean | never` in this example, which is reduced to `boolean`.

We will use `strictNullChecks` in the next chapters.

Creating tagged union types

With TypeScript 2.0, you can add a tag to union types and use these as type guards. That feature is called: **discriminated union types**. This sounds very difficult, but in practice it is very easy. The following example demonstrates it:

```
interface Circle {
  type: "circle";
  radius: number;
```

```
}
interface Square {
  type: "square";
  size: number;
}
type Shape = Circle | Square;
function area(shape: Shape) {
  if (shape.type === "circle") {
    return shape.radius * shape.radius * Math.PI;
  } else {
    return shape.size * shape.size;
  }
}
```

The condition in the `if` statements works as a type guard. It narrows the type of shape to `circle` in the `true` branch and `square` in the `false` branch.

To use this feature, you must create a union type of which all elements have a property with a string value. You can then compare that property with a string literal and use that as a type guard. You can also do that check in a switch statement, like the next example.

```
function area(shape: Shape) {
  switch (shape.type) {
    case "circle":
      return shape.radius * shape.radius * Math.PI;
    case "square":
      return shape.size * shape.size;
  }
}
```

We have now seen the new major features of the type system of TypeScript 2.0. We will see most of them in action in the next chapters. We will also write some simple algorithms in these chapters. We will learn some background information on writing and analyzing algorithms in the next section.

Comparing performance of algorithms

We will also write some small algorithms in the next chapters. This section shows how the performance of an algorithm can be estimated. During such analysis, it is often assumed that only a large input gives performance problems. The analysis will show how the running time scales when the input scales.

The next section requires some knowledge of basic mathematics. However, this section is not foreknowledge for the next chapters. If you do not understand a piece of this section, you can still follow the rest of the book.

For instance, if you want to find the index of an element in a list, you can use a for loop:

```
function indexOf(list: number[], item: number) {
  for (let i = 0; i < list.length; i++) {
    if (list[i] === item) return i;
  }
  return -1;
}
```

This `function` loops over all elements of the array. If the array has size n, then the body of the loop will be evaluated n times. We do not know how long the body of the loop runs. It could be hundreds or tens of a second, but that depends on the computer. When you run the program twice, the time will probably not be exactly the same.

Luckily, we do not need these numbers for the analysis. It is important to see that the running time of the body does not depend on the size of the array.

The `function` first sets i to , and then executes the code in the loop at most n times. In the worst case, the body is executed n times and the final `return -1` runs. The running time will then be `something + n * something + something`, where all instances of `something` do not depend on n. When the input is big enough, we can neglect the time of the initialization of i and the final `return -1`. So, for a large n, the running time is approximately `n * something`.

Big-Oh notation

Mathematicians created a notation to write this more simply, called Big-Oh notation. When you say that the running time is `O(n)`, you mean that the running time is at most n `*` `something`, for a big enough n. In general, `O(f(n))`, where `f(n)` is a formula, means that the running time is at most a multiple of `f(n)`. More formally, if you say that the running time is `O(f(n))`, you mean that for some numbers N and c the following holds: if n > N then the running time is at most c `*` `f(n)`. The condition n > N is a formal way of saying: if n is big enough, the value of c is the replacement of something.

For the original problem, this would result in O(n). When you analyze some other algorithms, you can count how often it can be executed for each piece of code. From these terms, you must choose the highest one. We will analyze the next example:

```
function hasDuplicate(items: number[]) {
  for (let i = 0; i < items.length; i++) {
    for (let j = 0; j < items.length; j++) {
      if (items[i] === items[j] && i !== j) return true;
    }
  }
  return false;
}
```

The first line, where i is declared, is only evaluated once. The line where j is declared is executed at most n times, because it is in the first for loop. The if statement runs at most n * n, or n^2 times. The last line is evaluated at most once. The highest term of these is n^2. Thus, this algorithm runs in O(n^2).

Optimizing algorithms

For a large array, this function might be too slow. If we would want to optimize this algorithm, we can make the second for loop shorter.

```
function hasDuplicate(items: number[]) {
  for (let i = 0; i < items.length; i++) {
    for (let j = 0; j < i; j++) {
      if (items[i] === items[j]) return true;
    }
  }
  return false;
}
```

With the old version, we would compare every two items twice, but now we compare them only once. We also can remove the check i !== j. It requires some more work to analyze this algorithm. The body of the second for loop is now evaluated 0 + 1 + 2 + ... + (n - 1) times. This is a sum of n terms and the average of the terms is (n - 1) / 2. This results in n * (n-1) / 2, or n2 / 2 - n / 2. With the Big-Oh notation, you can write this as O(n^2). This is the highest term, so the whole algorithm still runs in O(n^2). As you can see, there is no difference in the Big-Oh between the original and optimized versions. The algorithm will be about twice as fast, but if the original algorithm was way too slow, this one is probably too slow. Real optimization is a bit harder to find.

Binary search

We will first take a look at the `indexOf` example, which runs in `O(n)`. What if we knew that the input is always a sorted list? In such a case, we can find the index much faster. If the element at the center of the array is higher than the value that we search, we do not have to take a look at all elements on the right side of the array. If the value at the center is lower, then we can forget all elements on the left side. This is called **binary search**. We can implement this with two variables, `left` and `right`, which represent the section of the array in which we are searching: `left` is the first element of that section, and `right` is the first element after the section. So `right - 1` is the last element of the section. The code works as follows: it chooses the center of the section. If that element is the element that we search, we can stop. Otherwise, we check whether we should search on the left or right side. When `left` equals `right`, the section is empty. We will then return `-1`, since we did not find the element.

```
function binarySearch(items: number[], item: number) {
  let left = 0;
  let right = items.length;
  while (left < right) {
    const mid = Math.floor((left + right) / 2);
    if (item === items[mid]) {
    return mid;
    } else if (item < items[mid]) {
      right = mid;
    } else {
      left = mid + 1;
    }
  }
  return -1;
}
```

What is the running time of this algorithm? To find that, we must know how often the body of the loop is evaluated. Every time that the body is executed, the function returns, or the length of the section is approximately divided by two. In the worst case, the length of the section is constantly divided by two, until the section contains one element. That element is the searched element and the function returns or the length becomes zero and the function while loop stops. So, we can ask the question: how often can you divide n by two, until it becomes less than one? $^2\log$ n gives us that number. This algorithm runs in $O(^2\log(n))$, which is a lot faster than `O(n)`. However, it only works if the array is sorted.

In Big-Oh notation, $O(\log(n))$ and $O(^2\log(n))$ are the same. They only differ by some constant number, which disappears in Big-Oh notation.

Built-in functions

When you use other functions in your algorithm, you must be aware of their running time. We could for instance implement `indexOf` like this:

```
function fastIndexOf(items: number[], item: number) {
    items.sort();
    return binarySearch(items, item);
}
```

Both lines of the function are only executed once, but $O(1)$ is not the running time of this algorithm! This function calls `binarySearch`, and we know that the body of the while loop in that function runs, at most, approximately $^2\log\ n$ times. We do not need to know how the function is implemented, we only need to know that it takes $O(^2\log(n))$. We also call `.sort()` on the array. We have not written that function ourselves and we cannot analyze the code for it. For these functions, you must know (or look up) the running time. For sorting, that is $O(n\ ^2\log(n))$. So our `fastIndexOf` is not faster than the original version, as it runs in $O(n\ ^2\log(n))$.

We can however use sorting to improve the `hasDuplicate` function.

```
function hasDuplicate(items: number[]) {
    items.sort();
    for (let i = 1; i < items.length; i++) {
        if (items[i] === items[i - 1]) return true;
    }
    return false;
}
```

The loop costs $O(n)$ and the sorting costs $O(n\ ^2\log(n))$, so this algorithm runs in $O(n\ ^2\log(n))$. This is faster than our initial implementation, that took $O(n^2)$.

With this basic knowledge, you can analyze simple algorithms and compare their speeds for large inputs. In the next chapters, we will analyze some of the algorithms that we will write.

Summary

In this chapter, we have seen various new features of TypeScript 2.0. In this release, lots of new features for more accurate type analysis were added. We have seen control flow based type analysis, null and undefined checking, and tagged union types. Finally, we have also taken a look at analyzing algorithms. We will use most of these topics in the next three chapters. In Chapter 7, *Spreadsheet Application with Functional Programming*, we will build a spreadsheet application. We will also discover functional programming there.

7
Spreadsheet Applications with Functional Programming

In this chapter, we will explore a different style of programming: **functional programming**. With this style, functions should only return something and not have other side effects, such as assigning a global variable. We will explore this by building a spreadsheet application.

Users can write calculations in this application. The spreadsheet contains a grid and every field of the grid can contain an expression that will be calculated. Such expressions can contain constants (numbers), operations (such as addition, multiplying), and they can reference other fields of the spreadsheet. We will write a parser, that can convert the string representation of such expressions into a data structure. Afterwards, we can calculate the results of the expressions with that data structure. If necessary, we will show errors such as division by zero to the user.

Tax calculator

	0	1	2
0	Price without VAT	42	€
1	VAT percentage	21	%
2	VAT	8.82	€
3	Price with VAT	50.82	€

Add column

Add row

We will build this application using the following steps:

- Setting up the project
- Functional programming
- Using data types for expressions
- Writing unit tests
- Parsing an expression
- Defining the sheet
- Using the Flux architecture
- Creating actions
- Writing the view
- Advantages of Flux

Setting up the project

We start by installing the dependencies that we need in this chapter using NPM:

```
npm init -y
npm install react react-dom -save
npm install gulp gulp-typescript small --save-dev
```

We set up TypeScript with lib/tsconfig.json:

```
{
  "compilerOptions": {
    "target": "es5",
    "module": "commonjs",
    "noImplicitAny": true,
    "jsx": "react"
  }
}
```

We configure gulp in gulpfile.js:

```
var gulp = require("gulp");
var ts = require("gulp-typescript");
var small = require("small").gulp;

var tsProject = ts.createProject("lib/tsconfig.json");

gulp.task("compile", function() {
  return gulp.src(["lib/**/*.ts", "lib/**/*.tsx"])
    .pipe(ts(tsProject))
```

```
    .pipe(gulp.dest("dist"))
    .pipe(small("client/index.js", { externalResolve:
["node_modules"], outputFileName: { standalone: "client.js" }        }))
    .pipe(gulp.dest("static/scripts/"));
});
```

We install type definitions for React:

npm install @types/react @types/react-dom --save

In `static/index.html`, we create the HTML structure of our application:

```
<!DOCTYPE HTML>

<html>
  <head>
    <title>Chapter 5</title>
    <link href="style.css" rel="stylesheet" />
  </head>
  <body>
    <div id="wrapper"></div>
    <script type="text/javascript">
      var process = {
        env: {
          NODE_ENV: "DEBUG" // or "PRODUCTION"
        }
      };
    </script>
    <script type="text/javascript" src="scripts/client.js"></script>
  </body>
</html>
```

We add some basic styles in `static/style.css`. We will add more styles later on:

```
body {
  font-family: 'Trebuchet MS', 'Lucida Sans Unicode','Lucida Grande',
'Lucida Sans', Arial, sans-serif;
}

a:link, a:visited {
  color: #5a8bb8;
  text-decoration: none;
}
a:hover, a:active {
  color: #406486;
}
```

Functional programming

When you ask a developer what the definition of a function is, he would probably answer something like "something that does something with some arguments". Mathematicians have a formal definition for a function:

A function is a relation where an input has exactly one output.

This means that a function should always return the same output for the same input. **Functional programming** (**FP**) uses this mathematical definition. The following code would violate this definition:

```
let x = 1;
function f(y: number) {
  return x + y;
}

f(1);
x = 2;
f(1);
```

The first call to f would return 2, but the second would return 3. This is caused by the assignment to x, which is called a **side effect**. A reassignment to a variable or a property is called a side effect, since function calls can give different results after it.

It would be even worse if a function modified a variable that was defined outside of the function:

```
let x = 1;
function g(y: number) {
   x = y;
}
```

Code like this is hard to read or test. These mutations are called side effects. When a piece of code does not have side effects, it is called **pure**. With functional programming, all or most functions should be pure.

Calculating a factorial

We will take a look at the factorial function to see how we can surpass the limitations of functional programming. The factorial function, written as n! is defined as 1 * 2 * 3 * ... * n. This can be programmed with a simple for loop:

```
export function factorial(x: number) {
  let result = 1;
  for (let i = 1; i <= x; i++) {
    result *= i;
  }
  return result;
}
```

However, the value of i is increased in the loop, which is a reassignment and thus a side effect. With functional programming, recursion should be used instead of a loop. The factorial of x can be calculated using the factorial of x − 1 and multiplying it with x, since x! = x * (x−1)! for x > 1. The following function is pure and smaller than the iterative function. Calling a function from the same function is called recursion.

```
export function factorial(x: number): number {
  if (x <= 1) return 1;
  return x * factorial(x - 1);
}
```

 When you define a function with recursion, TypeScript cannot infer the return type. You have to specify the return type yourself in the function header.

We will use this function later on, so save this as lib/model/utils.ts.

Using data types for expressions

Fields of the spreadsheet can contain expressions, that can be calculated. To calculate these values, the input of the user must be converted to a data structure, which can then be used to calculate the result of that field.

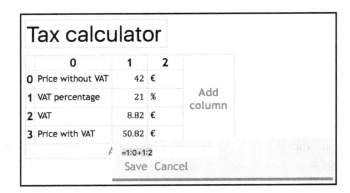

These expressions can contain constants, operations, references to other fields or a parenthesized expression:

- Constants: , `42`, `10.2`, `4e6`, `7.5e8`
- Unary expression: `-expression`, `expression!`
- Binary expression: `expression + expression`, `expression / expression`
- References: `3:1` (third column, first row)
- Parenthesized expression: `(expression)`

We will create these types in `lib/model/expression.ts`. First we import `factorial`, since we will need it later on.

```
import { factorial } from "./utils";
```

Creating data types

We can declare data types for these expression kinds. We define them using a class. We can distinguish these kinds easily using `instanceof`. We can declare `Constant` as follows:

```
export class Constant {
  constructor(
    public value: number
```

```
  ) {}
}
```

Adding public or private before a constructor argument is syntactic sugar for declaring the property and assigning to it in the constructor:

```
export class Constant {
  value: number;
  constructor(value: number) {
    this.value = value;
  }
}
```

A `UnaryExpression` has a kind (minus or factorial) and the operand on which it is working. We define the kind using an `enum`. For the expression, we reference the `Expression` type that we will define later on:

```
export class UnaryOperation {
  constructor(
    public expression: Expression,
    public kind: UnaryOperationKind
  ) {}
}
export enum UnaryOperationKind {
  Minus,
  Factorial
}
```

A binary expression also has a kind (`Add`, `Subtract`, `Multiply`, or `Divide`) and two operands.

```
export class BinaryOperation {
  constructor(
    public left: Expression,
    public right: Expression,
    public kind: BinaryOperationKind
  ) {}
}
export enum BinaryOperationKind {
  Add,
  Subtract,
  Multiply,
  Divide
}
```

We will call the reference to another field, a `Variable`. It contains the column and the row of the referenced field:

```
export class Variable {
  constructor(
    public column: number,
    public row: number
  ) {}
}
```

A parenthesized expression simply contains an expression:

```
export class Parenthesis {
  constructor(
    public expression: Expression
  ) {}
}
```

We can now define `Expression` as the union type of these classes:

```
export type Expression = Constant | UnaryOperation | BinaryOperation |
Variable | Parenthesis;
```

The preceding definition means that an `Expression` is a `Constant`, `UnaryExpression`, `BinaryExpression`, `Variable` or `Parenthesis`.

Traversing data types

We can distinguish these classes using `instanceof`. We will demonstrate that by writing a function that converts an expression to a string. TypeScript will change the type of a variable after an `instanceof` check. These checks are called type guards. In the code below, `formula instanceof Constant` narrows the type of `formula` to `Constant` in the block after the `if`. In the `else` block, `Constant` is removed from the type of `formula`, resulting in `UnaryOperation | BinaryOperation | Variable | Parenthesis`.

Using a sequence of `if` statements, we can distinguish all cases. For a constant, we can simply convert the value to a string:

```
export function expressionToString(formula: Expression): string {
  if (formula instanceof Constant) {
    return formula.value.toFixed();
```

For a `UnaryOperation`, we show the operator before or after the rest of the expression. We convert the rest to a string using recursion and we call `expressionToString` on the expression. Because of that, we had to specify the return type manually:

```
  } else if (formula instanceof UnaryOperation) {
    const { expression, kind } = formula;
    switch (kind) {
      case UnaryOperationKind.Factorial:
        return expressionToString(expression) + "!";
      case UnaryOperationKind.Minus:
        return "-" + expressionToString(expression);
    }
```

We convert a `BinaryOperation` to a string by inserting the operator between the converted operands:

```
  } else if (formula instanceof BinaryOperation) {
    const { left, right, kind } = formula;
    const leftString = expressionToString(left);
    const rightString = expressionToString(right);
    switch (kind) {
      case BinaryOperationKind.Add:
        return leftString + "+" + rightString;
      case BinaryOperationKind.Subtract:
        return leftString + "-" + rightString;
      case BinaryOperationKind.Multiply:
        return leftString + "*" + rightString;
      case BinaryOperationKind.Divide:
        return leftString + "/" + rightString;
    }
```

A variable is shown as the `column`, a `colon` and the `row`:

```
  } else if (formula instanceof Variable) {
    const { column, row } = formula;
    return column + ":" + row;
```

A parenthesized expression is shown as the containing expression wrapped in parentheses:

```
  } else if (formula instanceof Parenthesis) {
    const { expression } = formula;
    return "(" + expressionToString(expression) + ")";
  }
}
```

This function is a good example of walking through (traversing) a data structure with recursion. Such a function can be written in the following steps:

- Distinguish different cases (for instance using `instanceof` or `typeof`)
- Handle the containing nodes recursively (for instance, `left` and `right` of a `BinaryOperation`)
- Combine the results

In the next session, we will write another function that traverses an expression to validate it.

Validating an expression

When you are writing a function with recursion, you should always be sure that you are not creating infinite recursion, similar to an infinite loop. For instance, when you forget the base cases of the factorial function ($x <= 1$), you would get infinite recursion.

We would also get recursion when a field of the spreadsheet references itself (directly or indirectly). To prevent these issues, we will validate an expression before calculating it. We create the restriction that a reference should not point to itself and it may not reference a higher column or row index.

Later on, we will also show errors when a number is divided by zero, when the factorial of a negative or non-integer is calculated, when a referenced field contains an error, and when a referenced field contains text instead of a number. We define a class `Failure` to represent such an error:

```
export class Failure {
  constructor(
    public kind: FailureKind,
    public location: Expression
  ) {}
}
export enum FailureKind {
  ForwardReference,
  SelfReference,
  TextNotANumber,
  DivideByZero,
  FactorialNegative,
  FactorialNonInteger,
  FailedDependentRow
}
```

Next, we define a function which gives a string description of the error:

```
export function failureText({ kind }: Failure) {
  switch (kind) {
    case FailureKind.ForwardReference:
      return "This expression contains a forward reference to
another variable";
    case FailureKind.SelfReference:
      return "This expression references itself";
    case FailureKind.TextNotANumber:
      return "This expression references a field that does      not
contain a number";
    case FailureKind.DivideByZero:
      return "Cannot divide by zero";
    case FailureKind.FactorialNegative:
      return "Cannot compute the factorial of a negative number";
    case FailureKind.FactorialNonInteger:
      return "The factorial can only be computed of an integer";
    case FailureKind.FailedDependentRow:
      return "This expression references a field that has      one or
more errors";
  }
}
```

Now we can define a validate function, which will generate an array of errors. The function has two base cases: **constants** and **variables**.

A **constant** can never have errors. A **variable** is an error if it is a self or forward reference. For a unary, binary, or parenthesized expression we must validate the children recursively:

```
export function validate(column: number, row: number, formula: Expression):
Failure[] {
  if (formula instanceof UnaryOperation || formula instanceof Parenthesis)
{
    return validate(column, row, formula.expression);
  } else if (formula instanceof BinaryOperation) {
    return [
      ...validate(column, row, formula.left),
      ...validate(column, row, formula.right)
    ];
  } else if (formula instanceof Variable) {
    if (formula.column === column && formula.row === row) {
      return [new Failure(FailureKind.SelfReference, formula)];
    }
    if (formula.column > column || formula.row > row) {
      return [new Failure(FailureKind.ForwardReference, formula)];
    }
    return [];
```

```
    } else {
      return [];
    }
}
```

In the first `if` statement, the type of formula is `UnaryOperation | Parenthesis`. Since both types have the property `expression`, we can access it.

Calculating expressions

The last traversal is calculating the expression. This function will return a number if the calculation succeeded. Otherwise, it will return a list of errors. The arguments of the function are the expression and a function that gives the value of a referenced field:

```
export function calculateExpression(formula: Expression, resolve:
(variable: Variable) => number | Failure[]): number | Failure[] {
```

For a constant, we can simply return its value:

```
if (formula instanceof Constant) {
    return formula.value;
```

To calculate the value of a `UnaryOperation`, we first calculate its operand. If that contains an error, we propagate it. Otherwise, we calculate the factorial or the negative value of it. For a factorial we also show an error if it is not a non-negative integer. Because of the type guard, TypeScript narrows the type of `value` to a `number` in the `else` block:

```
    } else if (formula instanceof UnaryOperation) {
      const { expression, kind } = formula;
      const value = calculateExpression(expression, resolve);
      if (value instanceof Array) {
        return value;
      } else {
        switch (kind) {
          case UnaryOperationKind.Factorial:
            if (value < 0) {
              return [new              Failure(FailureKind.FactorialNegative,
    formula)];
            }
            if (Math.round(value) !== value) {
              return [new
    Failure(FailureKind.FactorialNonInteger, formula)];
            }
            return factorial(Math.round(value));
          case UnaryOperationKind.Minus:
            return -value;
```

```
      }
    }
```

For a binary operation, we calculate the left and right side. If one of these contains errors, we return those. Otherwise we apply the operator to both values:

```
} else if (formula instanceof BinaryOperation) {
  const { left, right, kind } = formula;
  const leftValue = calculateExpression(left, resolve);
  const rightValue = calculateExpression(right, resolve);
  if (leftValue instanceof Array) {
    if (rightValue instanceof Array) {
      return [...leftValue, ...rightValue];
    }
    return leftValue;
  } else if (rightValue instanceof Array) {
    return rightValue;
  } else {
    switch (kind) {
      case BinaryOperationKind.Add:
        return leftValue + rightValue;
      case BinaryOperationKind.Subtract:
        return leftValue - rightValue;
      case BinaryOperationKind.Multiply:
        return leftValue * rightValue;
      case BinaryOperationKind.Divide:
        if (rightValue === 0) {
          return [new              Failure(FailureKind.DivideByZero,
formula)];
        }
        return leftValue / rightValue;
    }
  }
```

For a variable, we delegate the calculation to the `resolve` function:

```
} else if (formula instanceof Variable) {
  return resolve(formula);
} else if (formula instanceof Parenthesis) {
  return calculateExpression(formula.expression, resolve);
}
}
```

Finally, we calculate the value of a parenthesized expression with the expression it contains.

Writing unit tests

Functional written code is usually easier to test with a unit test. A unit test is an automated test that checks whether a small piece of code is working. We will use the ava test runner, which we can install using NPM:

```
npm install ava --save-dev
npm install ava -g
```

At the time of writing, ava does not have type definitions bundled. We will quickly add some types for it in lib/test/ava.d.ts:

```
declare module "ava" {
  function test(name: string, run: (t: any) => void): void;
  namespace test {}
  export = test;
}
```

We can now write some tests for the factorial function. In lib/test/utils.ts, we write a test case. Any test file will have the following structure:

```
import * as test from "ava";
import { factorial } from "../model/utils";

test("factorial", t => {
  t.is(factorial(0), 1);
  t.is(factorial(1), 1);
  t.is(factorial(2), 2);
  t.is(factorial(3), 6);
  t.is(factorial(4), 24);
});
```

First, ava needs to be imported. Secondly, we must import the functions that we want to test. Finally, we create test cases. This file has one test case with five assertions. You can run the tests in a terminal:

```
gulp compile && ava dist/test
```

If some assertion fails, ava will show the exact location of the error.

We can also write tests for the functions in expression.ts. In lib/test/expression.ts, we add two tests which will test calculateExpression and expressionToString:

```
import * as test from "ava";
import { Expression, Constant, UnaryOperation, UnaryOperationKind,
```

```
BinaryOperation, BinaryOperationKind, Variable, calculateExpression,
expressionToString } from "../model/expression";

test("calculateExpression", t => {
  function testExpression(result: number, expression: Expression) {
    t.is(calculateExpression(expression, () => 1), result);
  }
  testExpression(5,
    new Constant(5));
  testExpression(-14,
    new UnaryOperation(new Constant(14),       UnaryOperationKind.Minus));
  testExpression(28,
    new BinaryOperation(new Constant(14),       new Constant(2),
BinaryOperationKind.Multiply));
  testExpression(1,
    new Variable(0, 0));
});
test("expressionToString", t => {
  function testString(result: string, expression: Expression) {
    t.is(expressionToString(expression), result);
  }
  testString("5",
    new Constant(5));
  testString("-14",
    new UnaryOperation(new Constant(14),       UnaryOperationKind.Minus));
  testString("14*2",
    new BinaryOperation(new Constant(14),       new Constant(2),
BinaryOperationKind.Multiply));
  testString("0:0",
    new Variable(0, 0));
});
```

Parsing an expression

A parser can convert a string to some data type. The first guess of the type of a parser would be:

```
type Parser<T> = (source: string) => T;
```

Since we will also use a parser to parse a part of the source. For instance, when parsing a factorial, we first parse the operand (which hopefully has one character remaining, the exclamation mark) and then parse the exclamation mark. Thus, a parser should return the resulting data and the remaining source:

```
type Parser<T> = (source: string) => [T, string];
```

A constant (such as 5.2) and a variable (5:2) both start with a number. Because of that, a parser should return an array with all options:

```
type Parser<T> = (source: string) => [T, string][];
```

To demonstrate how this works, imagine that there are two parsers: one that parses A, one that parses AA and one that parses AB. The string AAA could be parsed with a sequence of these parsers in three different ways: A-A-A, A-AA, and AA-A. Now imagine that the parsers can first parse A or AA, and then only AB. We will parse AAB. The first part would result in the following result:

```
[
  ["A", "AB"]
  ["AA", "B"]
]
```

The remaining string of the first element (AB), can then be parsed by the second parser (AB). This would have an empty string as the remaining part. The remaining string of the second item (B) cannot be parsed. Thus, these parses can parse AAB as A-AB.

Creating core parsers

We will first create two core parsers in `lib/model/parser.ts`. The function `parse` runs a parser and returns the result if successful, `epsilon` will always succeed and `token` will try to parse a specific string. The value can be specified as the last argument for both functions:

```
type ParseResult<T> = [T, string][];
type Parser<T> = (source: string) => ParseResult<T>;

export function parse<U>(parser: Parser<U>, source: string): U | undefined
{
    const result = parser(source)
        .filter(([result, rest]) => rest.length === 0)[0];
    if (!result) return undefined;
    return result[0];
}

const epsilon = <U>(value: U): Parser<U> => source =>
  [[value, source]];

const token = <U>(term: string, value: U): Parser<U> => source => {
  if (source.substring(0, term.length) === term) {
    return [[value, source.substring(term.length)]];
  } else {
    return [];
```

```
    }
};
```

We will combine these core parsers into more complex and useful parsers. First, we will create a function that tries different parsers:

```
const or = <U>(...parsers: Parser<U>[]): Parser<U> => source =>
    (<[U, string][]>[]).concat(...parsers.map(parser =>    parser(source)));
```

We can use this to parse a digit. We combine the parsers that parse the number 0 t0 9:

```
const parseDigit = or(
    token("0", 0), token("1", 1),
    token("2", 2), token("3", 3),
    token("4", 4), token("5", 5),
    token("6", 6), token("7", 7),
    token("8", 8), token("9", 9)
);
```

 Functions that have functions as an argument or return type are called **high order functions**. These functions can easily be reused. With functional programming, you often create such functions.

Running parsers in a sequence

Another way to combine parsers is running them in a sequence. Before we can write these functions, we must define two helper functions in lib/model/utils.ts. flatten will convert an array of arrays into an array. flatMap will first call map on the array and secondly flatten:

```
export function flatten<U>(source: U[][]) {
    return (<U[]>[]).concat(...source);
}
export function flatMap<U, V>(source: U[], callback: (value: U) => V[]):
V[] {
    return flatten(source.map(callback));
}
```

Back in `lib/model/parser.ts`, we define a map function, which can convert a `Parser<U>` to a `Parser<V>`:

```
const map = <U, V>(parser: Parser<U>, callback: (value: U) => V): Parser<V>
=> source =>
  parser(source).map<[V, string]>(([item, rest]) => [callback(item),
rest]);
```

We also define a bind function, which will run a parser after another parser:

```
const bind = <U, V>(parser: Parser<U>, callback: (value: U) => Parser<V>):
Parser<V> => source =>
  flatMap(parser(source), ([result, rest]) => callback(result)(rest));
```

With functional programming, the type of a function can sometimes already describe the implementation. When the implementation gives no type errors, the implementation is in most cases correct.

Next up, we create two functions that can run two or three parsers in a sequence and can combine the results of these parsers into a specific type:

```
const sequence2 = <U, V, W>(
  left: Parser<U>,
  right: Parser<V>,
  combine: (x: U, y: V) => W) =>
  bind(left, x => map(right, y => combine(x, y)));

const sequence3 = <U, V, W, T>(
  first: Parser<U>,
  second: Parser<V>,
  third: Parser<W>,
  combine: (x: U, y: V, z: W) => T) =>
  bind(first, x => sequence2(second, third,    (y, z) => combine(x, y,
z)));
```

With these functions, we can write a function that can match a sequence of any length, or a list. A list is either one element or one element followed by a list. As you can see, this requires recursion. We need the resulting parser inside the definition of the parser, which is not possible. Instead, we can create a function that will evaluate the parser (`source => parser(source)`):

```
function list<U>(parseItem: Parser<U>) {
  const parser: Parser<U[]> = or(
    map(parseItem, item => [item]),
    sequence2(
      parseItem,
      source => parser(source),
      (item, items) => [item, ...items]
    )
  );
  return parser;
}
```

We can also create a separated list parser, which will either parse only one element, or parse the first element and a list of separators and items. We create an interface to store the result of the function:

```
interface SeparatedList<U, V> {
  first: U;
  items: [V, U][];
}
const separatedList = <U, V>(parseItem: Parser<U>, parseSeparator:
Parser<V>) =>
  or(
    map(parseItem, first => ({ first, items: [] })),
    sequence2(
      parseItem,
      list(sequence2(parseSeparator, parseItem, (sep, item) => <[V,
U]>[sep, item])),
      (first, items) => ({ first, items })
    )
  );
```

We can now parse a list of digits:

```
const parseDigits = list(parseDigit);
```

This can parse a list of digits. We can convert that to a number with the `map` function that we have defined. Since an integer can be written as $1337 = 1 * 10^3 + 3 * 10^2 + 3 * 10^1 + 7 * 10^0$. We can use the `reduce` function of arrays for this. `reduce` works as follows: `[1, 2, 3, 4].reduce(f, 0) === f(f(f(f(0, 1), 2), 3), 4)`

We can now define the conversion function:

```
const toInteger = (digits: number[]) => digits.reduce(
  (previous, current, index) =>
    previous + current * Math.pow(10, digits.length - index - 1),
  0
);
```

With map, we can define `parseInteger`:

```
const parseInteger = map(parseDigits, toInteger);
```

A variable can be parsed as a sequence of an integer (the `column`), a colon, and another integer (the `row`):

```
const parseVariable = sequence3(parseInteger, token(":", undefined),
parseInteger,
  (column, separator, row) => new Variable(column, row));
```

Parsing a number

A number or constant can be written in the following ways:

- 8 (integer)
- 8.5 (with decimal part)
- 8e4 = 80000 (with exponent)
- 8.5e4 = 85000 (with decimal part and exponent)

We create two parsers, that will parse the decimal part and exponent of a number. They fallback to a default value (0 and 1) in case the number does not have a decimal part or exponent:

```
const parseDecimal = or(
  epsilon(0),
  sequence2(
    token(".", undefined),
    parseDigits,
    (dot, digits) => toInteger(digits) / Math.pow(10, digits.length)
  )
);
const parseExponent = or(
  epsilon(1),
  sequence2(
    token("e", undefined),
    parseDigits,
```

```
    (e, digits) => Math.pow(10, toInteger(digits))
  )
);
```

With these functions, we can easily define the `parseConstant` function:

```
const parseConstant = sequence3(
  parseInteger,
  parseDecimal,
  parseExponent,
  (int, decimal, exp) => new Constant((int + decimal) * exp)
);
```

We can now define a parser called `parseConstantVariableOrParenthesis`, which will parse a constant, variable, or parenthesized expression (as the name suggests). `parseParenthesis` will be implemented later on:

```
const parseConstantVariableOrParenthesis = or(parseConstant, parseVariable,
parseParenthesis);
```

Order of operations

When evaluating an expression, the order of execution is important. For instance, `(3 * 4) + 2` equals `14`, while `3 * (4 + 2)` equals `18`. The correct evaluation of `3 * 4 + 2` is the first one. An expression should be evaluated in this order:

1. Parenthesis
2. Multiplication and division
3. Addition and subtraction
4. Unary expressions

Multiple instances of the same group should be evaluated from left to right, so `10 - 2 + 3 = (10 - 2) + 3`.

Two ways exist to implement this: parsing the source in the right order, or parsing it left to right and correcting it during calculation. Since we already wrote the calculation part, we will parse the source in the right order. That is also the easiest option.

Based on these rules, the left or right side of a multiplication or division can never be an addition or subtraction. The operand of a unary expression can only be a constant, variable, or parenthesized expression. With these restrictions, one can create the following abstract representation:

```
Expression ← Term | Expression ('+' | '-') Term
Term ← Factor | Term ('*' | '/') Factor
Factor ← ConstantVariableOrParenthesis | '-' ConstantVariableOrParenthesis
| ConstantVariableOrParenthesis '!'
Parenthesis ← '(' Expression ')'
ConstantVariableOrParenthesis ← Constant | Variable | Parenthesis
```

This means that an expression is either a single term, or an addition and subtraction of multiple terms. A term is a factor or a multiplication and division of factors. A factor can be a constant, variable or parenthesized expression, optionally with a minus or an exclamation mark. With these rules, an expression will always be parsed in the right order.

We can easily convert this abstract representation to parsers. We start with `parseFactor`, which can be built with `or` and `sequence2`.

```
const parseFactor = or(
  parseConstantVariableOrParenthesis,
  sequence2(
    token("-", undefined),
    parseConstantVariableOrParenthesis,
    (t, value) => new UnaryOperation(value, UnaryOperationKind.Minus)
  ),
  sequence2(
    parseConstantVariableOrParenthesis,
    token("!", undefined),
    (value) => new UnaryOperation(value, UnaryOperationKind.Factorial)
  )
);
```

We can implement `parseTerm` and `parseExpression` using the function `seperatedList`. We will use reduce to transform the array into a `BinaryOperation`, just like we used it to convert an array of numbers into a single number in `toInteger`. First, we create the function that transforms the array into a `BinaryOperation`.

```
function foldBinaryOperations({ first, items }: SeparatedList<Expression,
BinaryOperationKind>) {
  return items.reduce(fold, first);

  function fold(previous: Expression, [kind, next]: [BinaryOperationKind,
Expression]) {
    return new BinaryOperation(previous, next, kind);
  }
}
```

We use that function in `parseTerm` and `parseExpression`.

```
const parseTerm = map(
```

```
    separatedList(
      parseFactor,
      or(
        token("*", BinaryOperationKind.Multiply),
        token("/", BinaryOperationKind.Divide)
      )
    ),
    foldBinaryOperations
);
export const parseExpression = map(
    separatedList(
      parseTerm,
      or(
        token("+", BinaryOperationKind.Add),
        token("-", BinaryOperationKind.Subtract)
      )
    ),
    foldBinaryOperations
);
```

We have not defined `parseParenthesis` yet. Because it depends on `parseExpression`, we must place it below its definition. However, if we would define it here with `const`, it cannot be referenced in `parseConstantVariableOrParenthesis`. Instead we will define it as a function.

```
function parseParenthesis(source: string): ParseResult<Expression> {
    return sequence3(
      token("(", undefined),
      parseExpression,
      token(")", undefined),
      (left, expression, right) => new Parenthesis(expression)
    )(source);
}
```

Functions can be used before their definition. We add the source as an argument, as defined in the `Parser` type.

Defining the sheet

A spreadsheet will be a grid of fields. Every field can contain a string or an expression, as demonstrated in the following screenshot:

In `lib/model/sheet.ts`, we will define the sheet and create functions to parse, show and calculate all expressions in the field.

First, we will import types and functions that we will use in this file.

```
import { Expression, Variable, calculateExpression, Constant, Failure,
FailureKind, validate, expressionToString } from "./expression";
import { parse, parseConstant, parseExpression} from "./parser";
```

We can define a field as an expression or a string, and a sheet as a grid of fields:

```
export type Field = Expression | string;
export class Sheet {
  constructor(
    public title: string,
    public grid: Field[][]
  ) {}
}
```

Now we will write functions that give the amount of columns and rows of the sheet.

```
export function columns(sheet: Sheet) {
  return sheet.grid.length;
}
export function rows(sheet: Sheet) {
  const firstColumn = sheet.grid[0];
  if (firstColumn) return firstColumn.length;
  return 0;
}
```

The user can write text or an expression in the fields of the spreadsheet. When the content of a field starts with an equals token, it is considered an expression. We write a function `parseField` that parses the content to an expression if it starts with the equals token. Otherwise, it will return the string as-is.

```
export function parseField(content: string): Field {
  if (content.charAt(0) === "=") {
    return parse(parseExpression, content.substring(1));
  } else {
    return content;
  }
}
```

We also create a function that changes a field to a string.

```
export function fieldToString(field: Field) {
  if (typeof field === "string") {
    return field;
  } else {
    return "=" + expressionToString(field);
  }
}
```

In case of an expression, it converts it to a string and adds an equals token before it. Otherwise, it just returns the string.

Calculating all fields

We will write a function that calculates all expressions in the spreadsheet. A field that contains an expression is converted to a number, if the calculation succeeded, or an array of errors otherwise. A field that contains text does not need calculation, so the content is immediately returned.

This yields this type for the result of the calculation:

```
export type Result = ResultField[][];
export type ResultField = string | number | Failure[];
```

We will use two nested loops to loop over each field. This is not pure, but it makes it easier to resolve variables in expressions. When a valid expression is to be calculated, the referenced fields would already be evaluated.

```
export function calculateSheet({ grid }: Sheet) {
  const result: ResultField[][] = [];

  for (let column = 0; column < grid.length; column++) {
    const columnContent = grid[column];
    result[column] = [];
    for (let row = 0; row < columnContent.length; row++) {
      result[column][row] = calculateField(column, row);
    }
```

```
    }

    return result;
```

For each field, we first check whether it is a string. If so, we can immediately return it. Otherwise, we validate the expression. If the expression is invalid, we return the errors and otherwise we run `calculateExpression` on it.

```
function calculateField(column: number, row: number): ResultField {
  const field = grid[column][row];
  if (typeof field === "string") {
    return field;
  } else {
    const errors = validate(column, row, field);
    if (errors.length !== 0) return errors;
    return calculateExpression(field, resolveVariable);
  }
}
```

When a variable reference needs to be resolved, we can access the calculated value from the array `result`. If it contains a string, we try to convert it to a number.

```
function resolveVariable(location: Variable): number | Failure[] {
  const { column, row } = location;
  const value = result[column][row];
  if (typeof value === "string") {
    const num = parse(parseConstant, value);
    if (num === undefined) {
      return [new Failure(FailureKind.TextNotANumber,
location)];
    }
    return num.value;
  } else if (value instanceof eArray) {
    return [new Failure(FailureKind.FailedDependentRow,
location)];
  } else {
    return value;
  }
}
```

We have already written a parser that can parse a constant, so we can reuse it here. If it contains an array of errors, we return a new error, which says that a referenced field contains an error. Otherwise, the field contains a number and we can simply return that.

Using the Flux architecture

In React, every class component can have a state. Maintaining a state is a side effect and not pure, so we will not use that in this application. Instead, we will use Stateless Functional Components, which are pure. We still need to maintain the state of the application. We will use the Flux architecture to do that. With Flux, you need to write a small piece of non-pure, but the other parts of the application can be written pure. The architecture can be divided into these parts:

- **Store**: Contains the state of the application
- **View**: React components that render the state to HTML
- **Action**: A function that can modify the state (example: rename the spreadsheet)
- **Dispatcher**: A hub modifies the state by executing an action

Several implementations of Flux exist. We will build our own, so that we can understand the ideas better and we can create an implementation that can be properly typed using TypeScript.

We will implement these parts in the following sections.

Defining the state

In `lib/model/state.ts`, we can define an interface that contains the state of the application. The state should contain this information:

- Active spreadsheet
- Calculated results of all expressions
- Selected column and row if a popup is opened
- Content of the textbox of the popup
- Whether or not the textbox of the popup contains a syntax error

This yields the following declaration:

```
import { Sheet, Result } from "./sheet";

export interface State {
  sheet: Sheet;
  result: Result;

  selectedColumn: number;
  selectedRow: number;
```

```
    popupInput: string;
    popupSyntaxError: boolean;
}
```

If the `popup` is not shown, we will set `selectedColumn` and `selectedRow` to `undefined`. Otherwise, these properties will contain the column and row of the selected field.

```
const emptyRow = ["", ""];
const emptyGrid = [
  emptyRow,
  emptyRow
]
export const emptySheet = new Sheet("Untitled", emptyGrid)

export const empty: State = {
  sheet: emptySheet,
  result: emptyGrid,

  selectedColumn: undefined,
  selectedRow: undefined,
  popupInput: "",
  popupSyntaxError: false
}
```

We should also construct the state of the application when it starts. It should contain an empty sheet and the popup should not be open.

Creating the store and dispatcher

We will create the store and dispatcher in `lib/model/store.ts`. The dispatcher should take an action and execute it. We first define an action as a function that modifies a state. Since we cannot assign to the state, as that is not pure, an action should not adjust the old state, but create a new state object with a certain modification.

```
export type Action<T> = (state: T) => T;
```

The dispatcher should accept such action. We define the dispatcher as a function with an action as an argument.

```
export type Dispatch<T> = (action: Action<T>) => void;
```

We can now create the store. The store should fire a callback when the state changes.

```
export function createStore<U>(state: U, onChange: (newState: U) => void) {
  const dispatch: Dispatch<U> = action => {
```

```
      state = action(state);
      onChange(state);
    }
    return dispatch;
  }
```

The store also needs an initial state. We add these two as arguments to the `createStore` function. The function will return the dispatcher.

Creating actions

An action should modify the state. To do that, we will first create three helper functions. One to modify a part of an object, one to modify a part of an array, and one to easily create a new array.

We use the same update function as we did in Chapter 3, *Note-Taking App with a Server*. We add this function to `lib/model/utils.ts`.

```
export function update<U extends V, V>(old: U, changes: V): U {
  const result = Object.create(Object.getPrototypeOf(old));
  for (const key of Object.keys(old)) {
    result[key] = (<any> old)[key];
  }
  for (const key of Object.keys(changes)) {
    result[key] = (<any> changes)[key];
  }
  return result;
}
```

We also create a function that changes the element at a certain `index` of an array. The other elements will remain at the same location. We will use this function to change the content of a field of the spreadsheet later on.

```
export function updateArray<U>(array: U[], index: number, item: U) {
  return [...array.slice(0, index), item, ...array.slice(index + 1)];
}
```

We define a function `rangeMap`, which creates an array. The callback argument is used to create each element of the array.

```
export function rangeMap<U>(start: number, end: number, callback: (index:
number) => U): U[] {
  const result: U[] = [];
  for (let i = start; i < end; i++) {
    result[i] = callback(i);
```

```
    }
    return result;
}
```

The functions `update` and `rangeMap` are not pure, since the functions contain several assignments. Sometimes it is not possible or very hard to write a function pure. However, these functions keep the side effects local and other functions will not perceive that the function is pure.

Adding a column or a row

In `lib/model/action.ts`, we will create the actions for our application. First we must import the types and function that we have written before.

```
import { State } from "./state";
import { calculateSheet, Field, rows, fieldToString, parseField } from
"./sheet";
import { update, updateArray, rangeMap } from "./utils";
```

Now we can create an action that calculates all expressions. We will not export this action, but we will use it in other actions.

```
const modifyResult = (state: State) =>
  update(state, {
    result: calculateSheet(state.sheet)
  });
```

With this definition, `modifyResult` is a function that takes a state and returns an updated state with a modified `result` property. This conforms to the Action type that we defined earlier.

We can use this function to create the actions that add a row or column. If a new row needs to be added, every column should get an extra field at the end. This field should be empty; it should contain the empty string. Afterwards, we need to update the `result` property of the state. We will use the `modifyResult` function for that.

```
export const addRow = (state: State) =>
  modifyResult(update(state, {
    sheet: update(state.sheet, {
      grid: state.sheet.grid.map(column => [...column, ""])
    })
  }));
```

To add a new column, we must add a new array with empty strings. We will use `rangeMap` to create such an array. We can use rows to get the amount of rows, and thus the length of the new array.

```
export const addColumn = (state: State) =>
  modifyResult(update(state, {
    sheet: update(state.sheet, {
      grid: [
        ...state.sheet.grid,
        rangeMap(0, rows(state.sheet), () => "")
      ]
    })
  }));
```

Later on, these actions can be triggered by `dispatch(addRow)` or `dispatch(addColumn)`. We will see that in action when we create the view.

Changing the title

Adding a row or a column is an action that does not have arguments. Changing the title does require an argument, namely the new title. Since the definition of an action does not allow extra arguments, we cannot write it as a function that requires the new title and the current state. Instead, we can create a function that takes the new title, and then returns a function that requires the current state. That will give this definition:

```
export const setTitle = (title: string) => (state: State) =>
  update(state, {
    sheet: update(state.sheet, { title })
  });
```

This action can be fired by running `dispatch(setTitle("Untitled"))`. If you forget the argument, or specify a wrong argument, TypeScript will give an error. Other implementations of Flux make it hard to type such actions.

Showing the input popup

We need to create several actions for the popup:

- Open the popup
- Close it
- Toggle it (close if it is already open, close it otherwise)
- Change the input of the textbox
- Save the new value

To open the popup, we need the column and the row of the field and save them in the state. We set the input of the popup to the content of that field, either a string or the expression converted to a string. When the popup is opened, it cannot have any syntax errors so we set that property to false.

```
export const popupOpen = (selectedColumn: number, selectedRow: number) =>
(state: State) =>
  update(state, {
    selectedColumn,
    selectedRow,
    popupInput:
fieldToString(state.sheet.grid[selectedColumn][selectedRow]),
    popupSyntaxError: false
  });
```

The popup can be closed by setting the column and row to undefined.

```
export const popupClose = (state: State) =>
  update(state, {
    selectedColumn: undefined,
    selectedRow: undefined,
    popupInput: ""
  });
```

To toggle the popup, we check whether it opened in the specified location, and close it or open it afterwards.

```
export const popupToggle = (column: number, row: number) => (state: State)
=>
  (column === state.selectedColumn && row === state.selectedRow)
    ? popupClose(state) : popupOpen(column, row)(state);
```

We can update the content of the input box:

```
export const popupChangeInput = (popupInput: string) => (state: State) =>
  update(state, {
    popupInput
  });
```

Finally, we can create an action that saves the input in the popup and closes it. However, when the popup contains a syntax error, we will not close the popup, but we will tell the user that the input contains an error. In such a case, `parseField` will return undefined. Otherwise, we change the field that is selected and recalculate the whole spreadsheet.

```
export const popupSave = (state: State) => {
  const input = state.popupInput;
  const value = parseField(input);
  if (value === undefined) {
    return update(state, {
      popupSyntaxError: true
    });
  }
  return modifyResult(update(state, {
    sheet: update(state.sheet, {
      grid: updateArray(state.sheet.grid, state.selectedColumn,
        updateArray(state.sheet.grid[state.selectedColumn],
state.selectedRow, value)
      )
    }),
    selectedColumn: undefined,
    selectedRow: undefined,
    popupInput: ""
  }));
};
```

These are all actions of our applications.

Testing actions

Since actions are pure functions, we can easily test them. They can be tested without the store, dispatcher, and view. To demonstrate this, we will write tests for addColumn, addRow and setTitle. We start with importing AVA, these functions and some helper functions.

```
import * as test from "ava";
import { empty } from "../model/state";
import { addColumn, addRow, setTitle } from "../model/action";
import { columns, rows } from "../model/sheet";
```

We will write a test for addColumn. We validate that the amount of columns is increased by one and that the amount of rows has not been changed.

```
test("addColumn", t => {
  const state = addColumn(empty);
  t.is(columns(state.sheet), columns(empty.sheet) + 1);
  t.is(rows(state.sheet), rows(empty.sheet));
});
```

We write a test for addRow too. This time, we validate that the amount of columns stayed the same but the amount of rows increased.

```
test("addRow", t => {
  const state = addRow(empty);
  t.is(columns(state.sheet), columns(empty.sheet));
  t.is(rows(state.sheet), rows(empty.sheet) + 1);
});
```

For setTitle, we check that the title has indeed been changed and that the grid has not changed.

```
test("setTitle", t => {
  const state = setTitle("foo")(empty);
  t.is(state.sheet.title, "foo");
  t.is(state.sheet.grid, empty.sheet.grid);
});
```

 When you get a bug report, try to create a unit test that demonstrates that error. When you have fixed the bug, you can easily validate it by running the tests and you prevent the bug from returning in the feature.

Writing the view

The application will show an input box at the top of the screen, which is used to type the title of the spreadsheet. Below the title, a table is shown which contains all fields of the spreadsheet. When the user clicks on a field, a popup is created which allows the user to change the content of that field. If the field contains errors, these errors are shown in the popup:

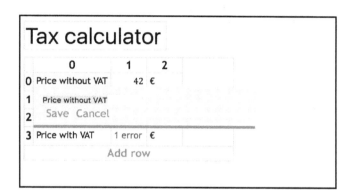

We will use React to create the view of our application. With Stateless Functional Components, we can write pure functions that render the state.

Rendering the grid

In `lib/client/sheet.tsx`, we will import React and functions and types that we created before:

```
import * as React from "react";
import { Dispatch } from "../model/store";
import { Expression, expressionToString, failureText } from
"../model/expression"
import { State } from "../model/state";
import { Sheet, Field, Result, ResultField, columns, rows, parseField,
fieldToString } from "../model/sheet";
import { update, rangeMap } from "../model/utils";
import * as action from "../model/action";
```

We will render the spreadsheet in `RenderSheet`. That function requires the `state` and the dispatcher.

```
export function RenderSheet({ state, dispatch }: { state: State, dispatch:
Dispatch<State> }) {
  const { sheet, result } = state;
  const columnCount = columns(sheet);
  const rowCount = rows(sheet);
```

At the top of the screen, we show the input box. When the user changes the title, we adjust the state to it with the `setTitle` action.

```
return (
  <div className="sheet">
    <input className="sheet-title" value={sheet.title}
      onChange={e => dispatch(action.setTitle((e.target as
HTMLInputElement).value))} />
```

We show the table below the title. In this table, we show the calculated values of all fields. We also show two buttons to add a new row or column. These buttons dispatch the actions that we defined earlier.

```
        <table>
          <tbody>
            <tr>
              <th></th>
              { rangeMap(0, columnCount, index => <th key={index}>{
index }</th>) }
              <th rowSpan={rowCount + 1}              className="sheet-add-
column">
                <a href="javascript:;"
                  onClick={() => dispatch(action.addColumn)}>Add
column</a>
              </th>
            </tr>
            { rangeMap(0, rowCount, renderRow) }
            <tr><th colSpan={columnCount + 2}>
              <a href="javascript:;"
                onClick={() => dispatch(action.addRow)}>Add row</a>
            </th></tr>
          </tbody>
        </table>
      </div>
    );
```

We render a row in the `renderRow` function. We use `rangeMap` to call this function, and to call `renderColumn`. React requires that we use the key property in a loop. We assign the `row` and `column` index to it, since these will be unique.

```
function renderRow(row: number) {
  return (
    <tr key={row}>
      <th>{ row }</th>
      { rangeMap(0, columnCount, renderColumn) }
    </tr>
  );
  function renderColumn(column: number) {
    return (
      <RenderField key={column} column={column} row={row}
state={state} dispatch={dispatch} />
    );
  }
}
```

React components should start with a capital letter. Normal functions should be named with a lower letter as a convention, but for components we have to break that rule.

Rendering a field

To render a field, we will first query the content of the field and check whether the popup is open on this field.

```
function RenderField({ column, row, state, dispatch }: {column: number,
row: number, state: State, dispatch: Dispatch<State> }) {
  const field = state.sheet.grid[column][row];
  const result = state.result[column][row];
  const open = state.selectedColumn === column
    && state.selectedRow === row;
```

Now we check whether the field contains text or an expression. In case of an expression, it can either be a successful calculation or a failed one. If it failed, we will show the amount of errors. In the popup, the user can read all errors. We generate a class name based on this, and on whether the popup is opened in this field.

```
let text: string;
let className: string;

if (typeof result === "string") {
  text = result;
  className = "field-string";
} else if (typeof result === "number") {
  text = result.toString();
  className = "field-value";
} else {
  text = result.length === 1 ? "1 error" : result.length +        "
errors";
  className = "field-error";
}
className += " field";
if (open) {
  className += " field-open";
}
```

With these variables, we can render the field. If we must show the popup, we will do that with `RenderPopup`.

```
return (
  <td className={className}>
    <span onClick={() => dispatch(action.popupToggle(column,
row))}>
      { text }
    </span>
    { open ?
      <RenderPopup
        field={field}
        content={result}
        syntaxError={state.popupSyntaxError}
        input={state.popupInput}
        dispatch={dispatch} />
      : undefined
    }
  </td>
);
}
```

We define that function in the next section. We attach an event listener to the field which will open or close the field when the user clicks on it.

Showing the popup

We will show the popup in `RenderPopup`. The popup contains an input box, a save, and cancel button:

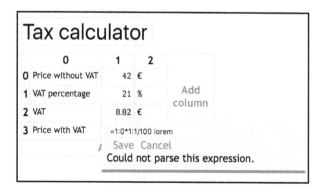

If the field contains an error, we show it below the two buttons:

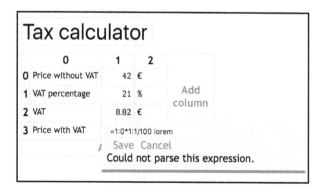

For errors other than syntax errors, we show the location where it happened:

We will first store all errors in a variable. In case of a syntax error, we cannot give details. For other errors, we show a description and the location of the error.

```
function RenderPopup({ field, content, syntaxError, input, dispatch }: {
field: Field, content: ResultField, syntaxError: boolean, input: string,
dispatch: Dispatch<State> }) {
  let errors: JSX.Element | JSX.Element[];
  if (syntaxError) {
    errors = <div className="failure">
      Could not parse this expression.
    </div>;
  } else if (content instanceof Array) {
    errors = content.map((failure, index) => <div className="failure"
key={index.toString()}>
      <span className="failure-text">{ failureText(failure) }</span>
      <span className="failure-source">{
expressionToString(failure.location) }</span>
    </div>);
  }
```

Now we can build the full view. We attach event listeners to the input box, save, and close button. We also wrap the input box in a form, such that the user can press *Enter* (instead of clicking **Save**) to accept the changes.

```
    return (
      <div className="field-popup">
        <form onSubmit={(e) => {e.preventDefault();
dispatch(action.popupSave);}}>
          <input value={input} autoFocus
            onChange={e => dispatch(action.popupChangeInput((e.target as
HTMLInputElement).value))} />
        </form>
        <a href="javascript:;" onClick={() =>
dispatch(action.popupSave)}>Save</a>
        <a href="javascript:;" onClick={() =>
dispatch(action.popupClose)}>Cancel</a>
        <br />
        { errors }
      </div>
    );
}
```

Adding styles

In `static/style.css`, we will add some more styles. We will make the text of the input box for the title bigger.

```
.sheet-title {
  font-size: 24pt;
  margin: 0 0 10px;
  border: 1px solid #ccc;
  width: 200px;
}
```

We will add a border to the table and style the button to add a column.

```
.sheet > table, .sheet tr, .sheet th, .sheet td {
  border: 1px solid #ccc;
  border-collapse: collapse;
}
.sheet-add-column > a {
  width: 70px;
  display: block;
}
```

We will style the fields so they show their value properly and can contain a popup.

```css
.field {
  position: relative;
}
.field > span {
  display: block;
  min-width: 42px;
  font-size: 10pt;
  height: 18px;
  padding: 3px;
}
.field-value > span {
  font-family: Cambria, Cochin, Georgia, Times, Times New Roman, serif;
  text-align: right;
}
.field-error > span {
  color: #aa2222;
}
.field-open {
  background-color: #eee;
}
```

We add some styles to the popup:

```css
.field-popup {
  position: absolute;
  left: 0px;
  top: 20px;
  z-index: 10;
  background-color: #eee;
  border-bottom: 4px solid #5a8bb8;
  border-right: 1px solid #ddd;
  padding: 8px;
  width: 300px;
}
.field-popup > input {
  margin-right: 10px;
}
.field-popup > a {
  margin-left: 10px;
}
```

Finally, we change the looks of error messages in the popup.

```
.failure-text {
  font-style: italic;
}
.failure-source {
  margin-left: 10px;
  color: #555;
  font-family: Cambria, Cochin, Georgia, Times, Times New Roman, serif;
}
```

Gluing everything together

In `lib/client/index.tsx`, we will combine all parts of our application. We will create a component that contains the state and renders the view. When the state is updated in the store, we will propagate that to this component and render the view again.

```
import * as React from "react";
import { render } from "react-dom";
import { createStore, Dispatch } from "../model/store";
import { State, empty } from "../model/state";
import { RenderSheet } from "./sheet";

class App extends React.Component<{}, State> {
  dispatch: Dispatch<State>;
  state = empty;

  constructor(props: {}) {
    super(props);
    this.dispatch = createStore(this.state,      state =>
this.setState(state));
  }
  render() {
    return (
      <div className="sheet">
        <RenderSheet
          state={this.state}
          dispatch={this.dispatch} />
      </div>
    );
  }
}
```

Finally, we can render this component in the HTML file.

```
render(<App />, document.getElementById("wrapper"));
```

We can view the result by running `gulp compile` and opening `static/index.html` in your browser.

Advantages of Flux

In this section you can find some of the advantages of using Flux, the architecture that we used in this chapter.

Flux is based on the unidirectional flow of data. Angular supports two way bindings, which allow data to flow in two directions. With this data flow, a lot of properties might get changed after a single change is made. This can lead to unpredictable behavior in big applications. Flow and React do not have such bindings, but instead there is a clean flow of data (`store | view | action | dispatch | store`).

The parts of Flux are not strictly bound to each other. This makes it easy to test specific parts of the application with unit tests. We already saw that the actions do not depend on the view.

Going cross-platform

Since the parts of Flux are not bound, we can, relatively, replace the HTML views of the application with views of a different platform. The user interface does not store the state of the application, but it is managed in the store. The other parts need no modification when the HTML views are replaced. This way we can port the application to a different platform and go cross-platform.

Summary

We have built a spreadsheet application with functional programming, React, and Flux in this chapter. We have discovered the limitations of functional programming and learned how we can take advantage of it. We have written automated unit tests for parts of the code that we have written. We also saw how we can traverse data structures and write a parser with functional programming. With the Flux architecture, we learnt how we can write the biggest part of the application with pure functions.

In the next chapter, we will see more of functional programming. We will rebuild Pac-Man with the HTML5 canvas.

8

Pac Man in HTML5

In this chapter, we will recreate Pac Man with the HTML5 canvas. Just like the previous chapter, we will be using functional programming. With the HTML5 canvas and JavaScript, you can play games in the browser.

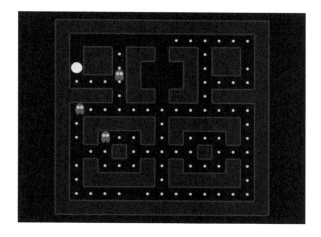

Pac Man is a classic game where the player (Pac Man, the yellow circle) must eat all of the dots. The ghosts are the enemies of Pac Man: when you get caught by a ghost, you lose. If you eat all of the dots without being caught by a ghost, you win the game.

Drawing on a canvas is, just like modifying the HTML elements of a page, a side effect and thus not pure. Since we will be using functional programming, we will create some abstraction around it, similar to what React does. We will build a small non-pure framework so we can use that to build the rest of the game with pure functions. We will also use strictNullChecks in this chapter. The compiler will check which values can be undefined or null.

We will build the game in these steps:

- Setting up the project
- Using the HTML5 canvas
- Designing the framework
- Drawing on the canvas
- Adding utility functions
- Creating the models
- Drawing the view
- Handling events
- Creating the time handler
- Running the game
- Adding a menu

Setting up the project

The project structure will be similar to the previous projects. In `lib`, we will place our sources. We separate the files for the framework and the game in `lib/framework` and `lib/game`. In `lib/tsconfig.json`, we configure TypeScript:

```json
{
    "compilerOptions": {
        "target": "es5",
        "module": "commonjs",
    "strictNullChecks": true
    }
}
```

In the root directory, we set up gulp in `gulpfile.js`:

```js
var gulp = require("gulp");
var ts = require("gulp-typescript");
var small = require("small").gulp;

var tsProject = ts.createProject("lib/tsconfig.json");

gulp.task("compile", function() {
   return gulp.src("lib/**/*.ts")
     .pipe(ts(tsProject))
     .pipe(small("game/index.js", { outputFileName: { standalone:
"scripts.js" }}))
     .pipe(gulp.dest("static/scripts/"));
```

```
});
gulp.task("default", ["compile"]);
```

We can install our dependencies with NPM.

```
npm init -y
npm install gulp gulp-typescript small --save-dev
```

Finally, we create a simple HTML file in `static/index.html`.

```
<!DOCTYPE HTML>
<html>
  <head>
    <title>Pac Man</title>
  </head>
  <body style="background-color: black;">
    <canvas id="game" width="800" height="600"></canvas>
    <script src="scripts/scripts.js"></script>
  </body>
</html>
```

Before we start writing the framework, we will have a quick look at how the HTML5 canvas works.

Using the HTML5 canvas

The **HTML5 canvas** is an HTML element, just like `<div>`. However, the canvas does not contain other HTML elements, but it can contain a drawing generated by JavaScript code. In `lib/game/index.ts` we will quickly experiment with it.

We can get a reference to the canvas using `document.getElementById` the same way we got a reference to a `<div>` element:

```
const canvas = <HTMLCanvasElement> document.getElementById("game");
```

We cannot directly draw on the canvas; we have to get a rendering context first. Currently, two kinds of rendering contexts exist: a two dimensional context and a `webgl` context, used for 3D rendering. The `webgl` context is a lot harder to use. Luckily, Pac Man is 2D, so we can use the 2D context:

```
const context = canvas.getContext("2d");
```

In an editor with completions, you can check which functions exist on the context. For instance, you can use `context.fillRect(10, 10, 100, 100)` to draw a filled rectangle from 10,10 to 110,110. The *x*-axis starts at the left side and goes to the right, and the *y*-axis starts at the top of the canvas and goes down.

Before you can draw anything on the canvas, you must set the drawing color. The canvas distinguishes two different color settings: the fill color and the stroke color. The fill color is used to paint a filled shape. The stroke color is used to draw a shape that only consists of an outline.

We can set these colors using `context.fillStyle` and `context.strokeStyle`:

```
context.fillStyle = "#ff0000";
context.strokeStyle = "#0000ff";
```

We can also set the weight of a line with a similar property.

```
context.lineWidth = 5;
```

We can draw rectangles with these styles.

```
context.fillRect(10, 10, 100, 100);
context.strokeRect(20, 20, 100, 100);
```

This results in the following image:

Saving and restoring the state

The context also has the functions `save()` and `restore()`. With these functions, you can restore the current draw styles, such as `fillStyle`, and `lineWidth`. `restore()` resets the state to the last time that `save()` was called, based on a LIFO stack (Last In, First Out).

In the following example, the restore on position 3 resets the state to the state saved on position 2, and `restore` on position 4 resets it to position 1:

```
context.save(); // 1
context.fillStyle = "#ff0000";
context.save(); // 2
context.strokeStyle = "#0000ff";
context.restore(); // 3
context.restore(); // 4
```

We will use these functions in the framework as they can easily be used with recursion.

Designing the framework

We will design the framework based on functional programming. The framework will do all non-pure work, so that the rest of the application can be built with pure functions (except for `Math.random`).

> Strictly speaking, `Math.random` is not a pure function. Given that `Math.random()` is not always equal to `Math.random()`, that function will update some internal state.
> In pure functional languages, such a function can still exist. That function takes a state and returns a random number and a new state. Since every call to random will get a different state, it can return different random values.

A game consists of an event loop. The amount of iterations that this loop does per second is called FPS or frames per second. Every step of the loop, the game state needs to be updated. For instance, enemies and the player can move, and the player can eat dots in Pac Man. At the end of each step, the game state must be redrawn.

The game must also handle user input. When the user presses the left button, the player should start moving to the left.

We will split the event loop into the following components:

- The view, which will draw the game every step
- A time handler, which will be called once in every step
- An event handler, which will be called for every event that occurs

With functional programming it can often be useful to think about the types of functions before you write them. We will take a quick look at the types of these three components. Imagine the state is stored in some interface `State`. The view will transform this state into a picture. The view might need the width and height of the canvas, so we add these as arguments. We will create the definition of a `Picture` later on:

```
function draw(state: State, width: number, height: number): Picture
```

The time handler should transform the state into a new state. It should not have any other arguments:

```
function timeHandler(state: State): State
```

The event handler also transforms the `state`, but it can use an extra argument, which contains the event that has occurred:

```
function eventHandler(state: State, event: Event): State
```

In the next sections, we will create a framework that manages these three components.

Creating pictures

We will start by creating data types for pictures. Some examples of a picture are a circle, a line, text, or a combination of those. Such pictures can also be scaled, repositioned (translated), or rotated. An empty picture is also a picture.

We define a picture as the union of these different kinds:

```
export type Picture
  = Empty
  | Rectangle
  | RectangleOutline
  | Circle
  | CircleOutline
  | Line
  | Text
  | Color
  | Translate
  | Rotate
  | Scale
  | Pictures;
```

We start by creating some basic types. The `Empty` picture can be defined as follows:

```
export class Empty {
  __emptyBrand: void;
}
```

This class does not need any properties. However, if you do not add any properties to a class, values of every type will be assignable to it. This is because TypeScript has a structural type system, and for instance a string has, at the least, all properties of an empty class (that is, no properties). For instance, a string or a number is assignable to that class. To prevent that, we add a **brand** to the class. A brand is a property that does not exist at runtime, but is used to prevent issues with structural typing.

For rectangles and circles, we create different types. One is filled, one has only the outline. For such outlines, we can set the thickness:

```
export class Rectangle {
  __rectangleBrand: void;

  constructor(
    public x = 0,
    public y = 0,
    public width = 1,
    public height = width
  ) {}
}
export class RectangleOutline {
  __rectangleOutlineBrand: void;

  constructor(
    public x = 0,
    public y = 0,
    public width = 1,
    public height = width,
    public thickness = 1
  ) {}
}
```

If we do not add a brand to these definitions, a `Rectangle` will be assignable to a `RectangleOutline`. These brands are also necessary to differentiate a rectangle and a circle:

```
export class Circle {
  __circleBrand: void;

  constructor(
    public x = 0,
    public y = 0,
    public width = 1,
    public height = width
  ) {}
}
export class CircleOutline {
  __circleOutlineBrand: void;

  constructor(
    public x = 0,
    public y = 0,
    public width = 1,
    public height = width,
    public thickness = 1
  ) {}
}
```

We define a line as a list of points and a thickness:

```
export type Point = [number, number];
export type Path = Point[];
export class Line {
  __lineBrand: void;

  constructor(
    public path: Path,
    public thickness: number
  ) {}
}
```

Next, we define the type for text:

```
export class Text {
  __textBrand: void;

  constructor(
    public text: string,
    public font: string
  ) {}
}
```

Wrapping other pictures

We can wrap other pictures and create new ones. For instance, we will change the color of a picture with Color. With this definition we can write new Color("#ff0000", new Circle(0, 0, 2, 2)) to get a red circle:

```
export class Color {
  __colorBrand: void;

  constructor(
    public color: string,
    public picture: Picture
  ) {}
}
```

We could also reposition a picture. This is usually called translating. new Translate(100, 100, new Circle(0, 0, 2, 2)) draws a circle around (100, 100) instead of (0, 0):

```
export class Translate {
  __translateBrand: void;

  constructor(
    public x: number,
    public y: number,
    public picture: Picture
  ) {}
}
```

As the name suggests, `Rotate` rotates some other picture:

```
export class Rotate {
  __rotateBrand: void;

  constructor(
    public angle: number,
    public picture: Picture
  ) {}
}
```

We can resize a picture with `Scale`. `new Scale(5, 5, new Circle(0, 0, 2, 2))` would draw a circle of 10×10 instead of 2×2:

```
export class Scale {
  __scaleBrand: void;

  constructor(
    public x: number,
    public y: number,
    public picture: Picture
  ) {}
}
```

The last class provides a way to show multiple pictures as one picture:

```
export class Pictures {
  __picturesBrand: void;

  constructor(
    public pictures: Picture[]
  ) {}
}
```

In `lib/framework/draw.ts`, we will draw these pictures on a canvas. We will implement that function later; we will now only define its header:

```
import { Picture, Rectangle, RectangleOutline, Circle, CircleOutline, Line,
Text, Color, Translate, Rotate, Scale, Pictures, Path } from "./picture";

export function drawPicture(context: CanvasRenderingContext2D, item:
Picture) { }
```

We have now defined all the data types needed to draw a picture. We will create events before we implement the `drawPicture` function.

Creating events

The application can accept keyboard events. We will distinguish between two kinds of event: a key press and a key release. We will not add mouse events, but you can add these yourself. We define these events in `lib/framework/event.ts`.

Every key has a certain key code, a number that identifies a key. For instance, the left arrow key has code 37. We will add the key code to the `event` class:

```
export const enum KeyEventKind {
  Press,
  Release
}
export class KeyEvent {
  constructor(
    public kind: KeyEventKind,
    public keyCode: number
  ) {}
}
```

We define the event source as a function that will be invoked every step. It will return a list of events that occurred in that step.

```
export function createEventSource(element: HTMLElement) {
  let queue: KeyEvent[] = [];

  const handleKeyEvent = (kind: KeyEventKind) => (e: KeyboardEvent) => {
    e.preventDefault();
    queue.push(new KeyEvent(
      kind,
      e.keyCode
    ));
  };
  const keypress = handleKeyEvent(KeyEventKind.Press);
  const keyup = handleKeyEvent(KeyEventKind.Release);
  element.addEventListener("keydown", keypress);
  element.addEventListener("keyup", keyup);
  function events() {
    const result = queue;
    queue = [];
    return result;
  }
  return events;
}
```

We will call this function in every step to check for new events. In the next section, we will pass these events to the event handler, which will update the game state.

Binding everything together

In `lib/framework/game.ts`, we will bind these components together. We will create a function that starts the event loop and updates the state every step. The function has these arguments:

- The canvas element on which the game will be drawn.
- The event element. Events on this element will be sent to the event handler. This does not have to be the same element as the canvas. An element needs focus to get keyboard events. Since the canvas does not always have focus, it can be better to listen for events on the body element, if there is only one game on the web page.
- The amount of frames per second.
- The initial state of the game.
- A function that draws the state.
- The time handler.
- The event handler.

We register the type of the state as a generic or type argument. Users of this function can provide their own type. TypeScript will automatically infer this type based on the value of the `state` argument:

```
import { Picture } from "./picture";
import { drawPicture } from "./draw";
import { createEventSource, KeyEvent } from "./event";

export function game<UState>(
  canvas: HTMLCanvasElement,
  eventElement: HTMLElement,
  fps: number,
  state: UState,
  drawState: (state: UState, width: number, height: number) => Picture,
  timeHandler: (state: UState) => UState = x => x,
  eventHandler: (state: UState, event: KeyEvent) => UState) {
```

With `createEventSource`, which we have written before, we can get an event source for the specified element:

```
const eventSource = createEventSource(eventElement);
```

To set up drawing, we must acquire the rendering context:

```
const context = canvas.getContext("2d")!;
```

The function `getContext` may return `null` when the context type is not supported. The type 2d is supported in all browsers that support a canvas, so we can safely cast it with an exclamation mark. This cast will remove the null ability from the type. We create an interval, such that the step function will be called multiple times per second, based on the `fps` parameter:

```
setInterval(step, 1000 / fps);
```

We will use the function `requestAnimationFrame` to render the view. This function takes a callback that will be called when the browser wants to redraw the page. If the browser does not need to redraw, or it has no time for it, it will not try to redraw it. If the draw function is pure, this does not affect the game:

```
let drawAnimationFrame = -1;
draw();

function step() {
  let previous = state;
  for (const event of eventSource()) {
    state = eventHandler(state, event);
  }
  state = timeHandler(state);
  if (previous !== state && drawAnimationFrame === -1) {
    drawAnimationFrame = requestAnimationFrame(draw);
  }
}
```

Finally, we create the draw function. This function renders the picture in the center of the screen. A canvas has an *x*-axis that goes to the left and a *y*-axis that goes down. In mathematics, however, the *y*-axis goes to the top. We will choose the latter and flip the whole picture. `context.restore();` will restore the state to the state at `context.save();`. The transformations do not influence any drawings after the draw function, for instance in the next step:

```
function draw() {
  drawAnimationFrame = -1;
  const { width, height } = canvas;

  context.clearRect(0, 0, width, height);

  context.save();
  context.translate(Math.round(width / 2), Math.round(height / 2));
  context.scale(1, -1);

  drawPicture(context, drawState(state, width, height));
```

```
      context.restore();
   }
}
```

We will use the save and restore function in the next section too. We will then draw all kinds of picture on the canvas.

Drawing on the canvas

In `lib/framework/draw.ts`, we will implement the `drawPicture` function that we created before. Using `instanceof` we can check which kind of picture we must draw.

We will interpret the location of an object as the center of it. Thus, `new Rectangle(10, 10, 100, 100)` will draw a rectangle around 10,10. We can draw the outline of a rectangle or the whole rectangle with `strokeRect` and `fillRect`:

```
import { Picture, Rectangle, RectangleOutline, Circle, CircleOutline, Line,
Text, Color, Translate, Rotate, Scale, Pictures, Path } from "./picture";

export function drawPicture(context: CanvasRenderingContext2D, item:
Picture) {
  context.save();
  if (item instanceof RectangleOutline) {
    const { x, y, width, height, thickness } = item;
    context.strokeRect(x - width / 2, y - height / 2, width, height);
  } else if (item instanceof Rectangle) {
    const { x, y, width, height } = item;
    context.fillRect(x - width / 2, y - height / 2, width, height);
```

To draw a circle, we use the arc function. That function does not draw the circle itself, but only registers its path. We can draw the line or fill it using stroke or fill. We must wrap `arc` with `beginPath` and `closePath` to do that:

```
  } else if (item instanceof CircleOutline || item instanceof Circle) {
    const { x, y, width, height } = item;
    if (width !== height) {
      context.scale(1, height / width);
    }
    context.beginPath();
    context.arc(x, y, width / 2, 0, Math.PI * 2);
    context.closePath();
    if (item instanceof CircleOutline) {
      context.lineWidth = item.thickness;
      context.stroke();
    } else {
```

```
    context.fill();
  }
```

For a line, we must do something similar. With `lineTo`, we can draw one section of the line. A line does not have to be closed; it does not have to end at the location it started. Thus, we do not call `closePath`:

```
  } else if (item instanceof Line) {
    const { path, thickness } = item;
    context.lineWidth = thickness;
    context.beginPath();
    if (path.length === 0) return;
    const [head, ...tail] = path;
    const [headX, headY] = head;
    context.moveTo(headX, headY);
    for (const [x, y] of tail) {
      context.lineTo(x, y);
    }
    context.stroke();
```

With `fillText`, we can draw text on the canvas. We will center the text. We must also scale the text, since we have flipped the whole canvas in `game.ts`. If you forget this, the text would be upside down:

```
  } else if (item instanceof Text) {
    const { text, font } = item;
    context.scale(1, -1);
    context.font = font;
    context.textAlign = "center";
    context.textBaseline = "middle";
    context.fillText(text, 0, 0);
```

We will draw pictures that contain other pictures, such as `Color` or `Pictures`, with recursion. For `Color`, we can simply set the color on the context:

```
  } else if (item instanceof Color) {
    const { color, picture } = item;
    context.fillStyle = color;
    context.strokeStyle = color;
    drawPicture(context, picture);
```

For `Translate`, `Rotate`, and `Scale`, we can use the `translate`, `rotate`, and `scale` functions that exist on the rendering context:

```
  } else if (item instanceof Translate) {
    const { x, y, picture } = item;
    context.translate(x, y);
```

```
    drawPicture(context, picture);
  } else if (item instanceof Rotate) {
    const { angle, picture } = item;
    context.rotate(angle);
    drawPicture(context, picture);
  } else if (item instanceof Scale) {
    const { x, y, picture } = item;
    context.scale(x, y);
    drawPicture(context, picture);
```

For `Pictures`, we can use a loop to render all pictures:

```
  } else if (item instanceof Pictures) {
    const { pictures } = item;
    for (const picture of pictures) {
      drawPicture(context, picture);
    }
  }
```

Finally, we restore the state of the context:

```
    context.restore();
}
```

We have now finished the work on the framework. We will develop the game in the next section.

Adding utility functions

We will write several utility functions in `lib/game/utils.ts`. With `flatten`, we will transform an array of arrays into one array.

```
export function flatten<U>(source: U[][]): U[] {
  return (<U[]>[]).concat(...source);
}
```

With update, we can modify some properties of an object. This is the same function as in previous chapters.

```
export function update<U extends V, V>(old: U, changes: V): U {
  const result = Object.create(Object.getPrototypeOf(old));
  for (const key of Object.keys(old)) {
    result[key] = (<any> old)[key];
  }
  for (const key of Object.keys(changes)) {
    result[key] = (<any> changes)[key];
```

```
  }
  return result;
}
```

Next, we will create a function for working with `Math.random`. `randomInt` will return a random integer in a certain range and `chance` has a chance to return `true`:

```
export function randomInt(min: number, max: number) {
  return min + Math.floor(Math.round(
    Math.random() * (max - min + 1)
  ));
}
export function chance(x: number) {
  return Math.random() < x;
}
```

We can calculate the difference between two points with the Pythagorean theorem:

```
export function square(x: number) {
  return x * x;
}
export function distance(x1: number, y1: number, x2: number, y2: number) {
  return Math.sqrt(square(x1 - x2) + square(y1 - y2));
}
```

Finally, we write a function that checks whether a number is an integer:

```
export function isInt(x: number) {
  return Math.abs(Math.round(x) - x) < 0.001;
}
```

Due to rounding errors, we must check that the value is near an integer.

Creating the models

In `lib/game/model.ts`, we will create the models for the game. These models will contain the state of the game, such as the location of the enemies, walls, and dots. The state must also contain the current movement of the player and the difficulty level, as the game will have multiple difficulties.

Using enums

We start with several enums. We can store the difficulty with such an enum:

```
export enum Difficulty {
    Easy,
    Hard,
    Extreme
}
```

The values of an enum are converted to numbers during compilation. TypeScript gives the first element zero as the value, the next item one, and so on. In this example, Easy is 0, Hard is 1, and Extreme is 2. However, you can also provide other values. For some applications, this can be useful. We will use custom values to define Movement. This enum contains the four directions in which the player can move. In case the user does not move, we use None. We give the members a value:

```
export enum Movement {
    None = 0,
    Left = 1,
    Right = -1,
    Top = 2,
    Bottom = -2
}
```

With these values, we can easily create a function that checks whether two movements are in the opposite direction: their sum should equal zero:

```
export function isOppositeMovement(a: Movement, b: Movement) {
    return a + b === 0;
}
```

Other useful patterns that are often used are bitwise values. A number is stored in a computer as multiple bits. For instance, 00000011 (binary) equals 3 (decimal). You can calculate the decimal value of a binary number as follows. The first position from the right has value 1. The next has value 2, then 4, 8, and so on. Summing the values of the positions with a one results in the decimal value.

You can use this binary representation to store multiple Booleans in a number. 00000011 would then mean that the first two values are true, and the other values are 0. We use an enum to define the names of these properties. << is the bitwise shift operator. 1 << x means that 00000001 is shifted x bits to the left. For instance, 1 << 4 results in 00010000:

```
export enum Side {
    Left = 1 << 0,
    Right = 1 << 1,
```

```
    Top = 1 << 2,
    Bottom = 1 << 3,
    LeftTop = 1 << 4,
    RightTop = 1 << 5,
    LeftBottom = 1 << 6,
    RightBottom = 1 << 7
}
```

We can combine multiple values using the bitwise or operator, |. A bit of the output is 1 if at least one of the input bits on that position is 1. Thus, Side.Left | Side.Right equals 00000011. We can check whether some bit is true with the bitwise and operator, &. A bit of the output of this operator is 1 if both input bits on that position are 1. For instance, 00000011 and Side.Right results in 00000010. This is not zero, so the Boolean value of Side.Right in that number is true.

We will use this later on to draw the edges of the walls. As you can see in the following screenshot, the edges of all walls are drawn.

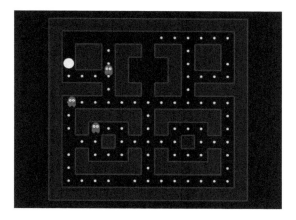

Storing the level

Now, we will define a model that can store the state of a level. A level contains several objects that are placed in a certain location:

```
export interface Object {
    x: number;
    y: number;
}
```

An enemy should also contain the location at which it is targeted. An enemy might not always know where the player is, so it cannot always run toward the player:

```
export interface Enemy extends Object {
  toX: number;
  toY: number;
}
```

For a wall, we store the sides on which walls exist. These neighbors are used to draw the walls:

```
export interface Wall extends Object {
  neighbours: Side;
}
```

We can store these objects in the level. We also store the size of the grid, the current movement and the movement based on the keyboard input in the level:

```
export interface Level {
  walls: Wall[];
  dots: Object[];
  enemies: Enemy[];
  player: Object;
  width: number;
  height: number;
  inputMovement: Movement;
  currentMovement: Movement;
  difficulty: Difficulty;
}
```

Creating the default level

We will write a function that can parse a level, based on a string. This allows us to create the level as follows:

```
const defaultLevel = parseLevel([
  "WWWWWWWWWWWWWWW",
  "W....E........W",
  "W.WWWWW.WWWWW.W",
  "W.W...W.W...W.W",
  "WE..W.....W...W",
  "W.W...W.W...W.W",
  "W.WWWWW.WWWWW.W",
  "W............W",
  "WWWW.WW WW.WWWW",
  "W....W   W....W",
```

```
    "W.WW.W P W.WW.W",
    "W.WW.WW WW.WWEW",
    "W............W",
    "WWWWWWWWWWWWWW"
]);
```

A W means that there should be a wall in that location, E stands for an enemy, P for the player, and a dot for a dot that Pac Man can eat.

To parse a level, we will first split these strings into an array of arrays, our grid:

```
function parseLevel(data: string[]): Level {
  const grid = data.map(row => row.split(""));
```

We will create a function mapBoard, which will transform this grid into an array of objects. toObject creates an object if the grid contains the specified character in that location:

```
return {
  walls: mapBoard(toWall),
  dots: mapBoard(toObject(".")),
  enemies: mapBoard(toEnemy),
  player: mapBoard(toObject("P"))[0],
  width: grid[0].length,
  height: grid.length,
  inputMovement: Movement.None,
  currentMovement: Movement.None,
  difficulty: Difficulty.Easy
};
```

In mapBoard, we first apply the callback to each element of the grid. We then flatten the grid to a one dimensional array. We filter elements that are undefined out of this array, as the callback should return undefined when the element in the grid at that location is not the expected kind:

```
function mapBoard<U>(callback: (field: string, x: number, y: number) => U |
undefined): U[] {
  const mapped = grid.map((row, y) => row.map((field, x) =>
  callback(field, x, y)));
  return flatten(mapped).filter(item => item !== undefined)
  as U[];
}
```

We have to cast the value in the return-statement. The TypeScript compiler cannot follow that the call to filter only passes through values that are not undefined.

In `toObject`, we create a function that will create an object if the grid contains the specified character at that position. A function that returns a function can be used to curry. Currying means that you first provide some arguments, and later on the other arguments. In this case, we provide the first argument, the kind within the `return` statement, some preceding lines. The other arguments are provided by the `mapBoard` function:

```
function toObject(kind: string) {
    return (value: string, x: number, y: number) => {
      if (value !== kind) return undefined;
      return { x, y };
    } We will return the content of a field of the grid in get. If the
index is out of bounds, we


    }
```

We will return the content of a field of the grid in `get`. If the index is out of bounds, we return `undefined`:

```
function get(x: number, y: number) {
    const row = grid[y];
    if (!row) return undefined;
    return row[x];
}
```

We use this function to check for the neighbors of a wall. Using the bitwise defined `enum`, we can register all sides on which the wall has a neighbor:

```
function toWall(kind: string, x: number, y: number): Wall | undefined {
    if (kind !== "W") return undefined;
    let neighbours: Side = 0;
    if (get(x - 1, y) === "W") neighbours |= Side.Left;
    if (get(x + 1, y) === "W") neighbours |= Side.Right;
    if (get(x, y - 1) === "W") neighbours |= Side.Bottom;
    if (get(x, y + 1) === "W") neighbours |= Side.Top;
    if (get(x - 1, y - 1) === "W") neighbours |= Side.LeftBottom;
    if (get(x - 1, y + 1) === "W") neighbours |= Side.LeftTop;
    if (get(x + 1, y - 1) === "W") neighbours |= Side.RightBottom;
    if (get(x + 1, y + 1) === "W") neighbours |= Side.RightTop;
    return {
      x,
      y,
      neighbours
    }
}
```

In `toEnemy`, we set the initial location of the enemy and the target location to the same values:

```
function toEnemy(kind: string, x: number, y: number) {
  if (kind !== "E") return undefined;
  return {
    x,
    y,
    toX: x,
    toY: y
  };
}
```

Finally, we create a small function that checks whether an object is aligned on the grid:

```
export function onGrid({ x, y }: Object) {
  return isInt(x) && isInt(y);
}
```

We have now created the default level. You can easily add another level later on, when the main menu has been added.

Creating the state

We store the state in a new interface. We will also define the default state for our game:

```
export interface State {
  level: Level;
}
export const defaultState: State = {
  level: defaultLevel
};
```

This interface is, at the moment, not very useful as you might be better off using the `Level` as the game state. However, later on in this chapter, we will also add a menu that should exist in the state.

Drawing the view

In `lib/game/view.ts`, we will render the game. We start with importing types that we defined earlier:

```
import { State, Level, Object, Wall, Side, Menu } from "./model";
import { Picture, Pictures, Translate, Scale, Rotate, Rectangle, Line,
Circle, Color, Text, Empty } from "../framework/picture";
```

We will store the font name in a variable, so we can easily change it later:

```
const font = "Arial";
```

In draw, we will render the game. For now, that means only drawing the level. Later on, we will add a menu to the game:

```
export function draw(state: State, width: number, height: number) {
  drawLevel(state.level, width, height),
}
```

We render the level in `drawLevel`. We calculate the size of all objects with the size of the grid and the canvas:

```
function drawLevel(level: Level, width: number, height: number) {
  const scale = Math.min(width / (level.width + 1), height / (level.height
+ 1));
```

We `scale` and `center` the whole level with this calculated scale:

```
  return new Scale(scale, scale,
    new Translate(-level.width / 2 + 0.5, -level.height / 2 + 0.5, new
Pictures([
```

Next, we draw all objects on the canvas. We use several functions that we create as follows:

```
      drawObjects(level.walls, drawWall),
      drawObjects(level.walls, drawWallLines),
      drawObjects(level.dots, drawDot),
      drawObjects(level.enemies, drawEnemy),
      drawObject(drawPlayer)(level.player)
    ]))
  );
```

In `drawObject`, we draw an object using the specified callback. We translate the picture of the object to the right location:

```
function drawObject<U extends Object>(callback: (item: U) => Picture) {
  return (item: U) =>
    new Translate(item.x, item.y, callback(item));
}
```

With `drawObjects`, we can draw a list of objects:

```
function drawObjects<U extends Object>(items: U[], callback: (item: U) =>
Picture) {
    return new Pictures(items.map(drawObject(callback)));
  }
}
```

In `drawWall`, we render the background of a wall:

```
function drawWall() {
  return new Color("#111", new Rectangle(0, 0, 1, 1));
}
```

We render the edges of a wall in `drawWallLines`. We check the neighbors of a wall with the bitwise `enum` that we defined earlier. First, we list all possible sides in an array:

```
const leftTop: [number, number] = [-0.5, 0.5];
const leftBottom: [number, number] = [-0.5, -0.5];
const rightTop: [number, number] = [0.5, 0.5];
const rightBottom: [number, number] = [0.5, -0.5];
const wallLines: [Side, Line][] = [
  [Side.Left, new Line([leftTop, leftBottom], 0.1)],
  [Side.Right, new Line([rightTop, rightBottom], 0.1)],
  [Side.Top, new Line([leftTop, rightTop], 0.1)],
  [Side.Bottom, new Line([leftBottom, rightBottom], 0.1)]
];
```

We filter this array with the bitwise `enum`, and `color` the remaining pieces:

```
function drawWallLines({ neighbours }: Wall) {
  const lines = wallLines
    .filter(([side]) => (side & neighbours) === 0)
    .map(([side, line]) => line);
  return new Color("#0021b3", new Pictures(lines));
}
```

In `drawDot`, we will show a small circle for a dot:

```
function drawDot() {
  return new Color("#f0c0a8", new Circle(0, 0, 0.2, 0.2));
}
```

We render the player as a circle. You can try to create the famous, eating Pac Man yourself later on:

```
function drawPlayer() {
  return new Color("#ffff00", new Circle(0, 0, 0.8, 0.8));
}
```

We do some more work to draw an enemy. The enemy will look as follows:

The background of the enemy consists of a circle for its head, a rectangle for the body, and two rotated rectangles for the feet.

```
function drawEnemy() {
  const shape = new Color("#ff0000", new Pictures([
    new Circle(0, 0.15, 0.6),
    new Rectangle(0, -0.05, 0.6, 0.4),
    new Translate(-0.15, -0.25,
      new Rotate(Math.PI / 4, new Rectangle(0, 0, 0.2, Math.SQRT2 *
0.15))),
    new Translate(0.15, -0.25,
      new Rotate(Math.PI / 4, new Rectangle(0, 0, 0.2, Math.SQRT2 * 0.15)))
  ]));
```

The eyes consist of two white circles with two smaller black circles as pupils.

```
    const eyes = new Color("#fff", new Pictures([
      new Circle(-0.12, 0.15, 0.2),
      new Circle(0.12, 0.15, 0.2)
    ]));
    const pupils = new Color("#000", new Pictures([
      new Circle(-0.12, 0.15, 0.06),
      new Circle(0.12, 0.15, 0.06)
    ]));
    return new Pictures([shape, eyes, pupils]);
}
```

Handling events

We will create an event handler in `lib/game/event.ts`. The event handler must set the correct movement direction in the state. The time handler will then use this to update the direction of the player. The step can only do that when the player is aligned to the grid. If the player is between two fields on the grid, we will not change the direction of the player, since he will then probably head into a wall.

Working with key codes

An event provides the key code of the pressed or released key. We can get this code of a certain character with `"x".charCodeAt(0)` (where x is the character). The key codes of left, top, right, and bottom are 37, 38, 39, and 40.

First, we must create a helper function that transforms a key code to the Movement `enum` that we defined earlier. We store the different keys that we use in a new `enum`:

```
import { KeyEvent, KeyEventKind } from "../framework/event";
import { State, Movement } from "./model";
import { update } from "./utils";

enum Keys {
  Top = 38,
  Left = 37,
  Bottom = 40,
  Right = 39,
  Space = " ".charCodeAt(0)
}
```

Now we can transform a key code to a `Movement`:

```
function getMovement(key: number) {
  switch (key) {
    case Keys.Top:
      return Movement.Top;
    case Keys.Left:
      return Movement.Left;
    case Keys.Bottom:
      return Movement.Bottom;
    case Keys.Right:
      return Movement.Right;
  }
  return undefined;
}
```

The event handler will invoke `eventHandlerPlaying`, which we will define later on in this section. When we add a menu to the application, we will adjust this handler:

```
export function eventHandler(state: State, event: KeyEvent) {
  return eventHandlerPlaying(state, event);
}
```

In `eventHandlerPlaying`, we update the movement in the state. When the user presses a key, we set the movement to that corresponding direction. When the user releases the key that maps to the current movement, we set the movement to `None`:

```
function eventHandlerPlaying(state: State, event: KeyEvent) {
  if (event instanceof KeyEvent) {
    const inputMovement = getMovement(event.keyCode);
    if (event.kind === KeyEventKind.Press) {
      if (inputMovement) {
        return update(state, {
          level: update(state.level, { inputMovement })
        });
      }
    } else {
      if (inputMovement === state.level.inputMovement) {
        return update(state, {
          level: update(state.level, { inputMovement: Movement.None })
        });
      }
    }
  }
  return state;
}
```

We have now finished the event handler for the game. When the user presses or releases a key, this is updated in the `state`. However, the real work is being done in the time handler, which we create in the next section.

Creating the time handler

The time handler requires some more work. First, we import other types and functions.

```
import { State, Level, Object, Enemy, Wall, Movement, isOppositeMovement,
onGrid, Difficulty } from "./model";
import { update, randomInt, chance, distance, isInt } from "./utils";
```

We define a `step` function so that we can add the `menu` later on.

```
export function step(state: State) {
  return stepLevel(state);
}
```

In `stepLevel`, we can update the objects in the level. First, we update the location of the enemies. We use `stepEnemy`, which we define later on.

```
function stepLevel(state: State): State {
  const level = state.level;
  const enemies = level.enemies.map(enemy => stepEnemy(enemy, level.player,
level.walls, level.difficulty));
```

We update the location of the player based on the current movement:

```
  const player = stepPlayer(level.player, level.currentMovement,
level.walls);
```

Dots that are near the player, are eaten by the player and removed from the level:

```
  const dots = stepDots(level.dots, player);
```

We change the current movement if the player is aligned on the grid or when they wants to move in the opposite direction:

```
  const currentMovement = onGrid(player) ||
isOppositeMovement(level.inputMovement, level.currentMovement) ?
level.inputMovement : level.currentMovement;
```

We use these values to update the level:

```
const newLevel = update(level, { enemies, dots, player, currentMovement
});
  return update(state, { level: newLevel });
}
```

Now, we create a function that checks whether an object collides with a wall:

```
function collidesWall(x: number, y: number, walls: Wall[]) {
  for (const wall of walls) {
    if (Math.abs(wall.x - x) < 1 && Math.abs(wall.y - y) < 1) {
      return true;
    }
  }
  return false;
}
```

Next, we create a function that updates the position of an enemy. The enemy can walk 0.0125 points if the difficulty is easy, otherwise,they can move 0.025 point. These values are chosen so that after a certain amount of steps, the enemy has walked exactly 1 point on the grid. Thus, the enemy will always be aligned to the grid again:

```
function stepEnemy(enemy: Enemy, player: Object, walls: Wall[], difficulty:
Difficulty): Enemy {
  const enemyStepSize = difficulty === Difficulty.Easy ? 0.0125 : 0.025;

  let { x, y, toX, toY } = enemy;
```

With a certain chance, the enemy will target on the player again. An enemy cannot always see where the player is, and the chance simulates that. Also, the enemy will get a small deviation:

```
if (chance(1 / (difficulty === Difficulty.Extreme ? 30 : 10))) {
  toX = Math.round(player.x) + randomInt(-2, 2);
  toY = Math.round(player.y) + randomInt(-2, 2);
}
```

If the enemy is aligned on the grid, it can move in all directions. Otherwise, it can only walk ahead or back:

```
if (!isInt(x)) {
  x += toX > x ? enemyStepSize : -enemyStepSize;
} else if (!isInt(y)) {
  y += toY > y ? enemyStepSize : -enemyStepSize;
} else {
```

The player is aligned on the grid, but the location might have a small rounding error. Thus, we round the values here.

```
x = Math.round(x);
y = Math.round(y);
```

To walk around, we first create an array of all options. Then, we filter these options and sort them. With a chance of 0.2, the enemy will choose the second-best option. Otherwise, it will choose the best option. The best option is the option that brings the enemy as close to the enemy:

```
const options: [number, number][] = [
  [x + enemyStepSize, y],
  [x - enemyStepSize, y],
  [x, y + enemyStepSize],
  [x, y - enemyStepSize]
];
const possible = options
  .filter(([x, y]) => !collidesWall(x, y, walls))
  .sort(compareDistance);
if (possible.length !== 0) {
  if (possible.length > 1 && chance(0.2)) {
    [x, y] = possible[1];
  }
  [x, y] = possible[0];
}
}
return {
  x, y, toX, toY
};
```

At the end of this function, we define the `compare` function that we used to sort the array. Such `compare` functions should return a negative value if the first argument comes after the second argument, and a positive value if the first argument should come before the other:

```
function compareDistance([x1, y1]: [number, number], [x2, y2]: [number,
number]) {
  return distance(toX, toY, x1, y1) - distance(toX, toY, x2, y2);
}
}
```

We update the location of the player in `stepPlayer`:

```
const playerStepSize = 0.04;
function stepPlayer(player: Object, movement: Movement, walls: Wall[]):
Object {
  let { x, y } = player;
```

When the player is aligned on the grid, we round the location to eliminate rounding errors:

```
if (onGrid(player)) {
  x = Math.round(x);
  y = Math.round(y);
}
```

If the user has no movement, we do not modify the player and we can return it directly:

```
switch (movement) {
  case Movement.None:
    return player;
```

Otherwise, we update the x or y coordinate of the player:

```
case Movement.Left:
  x -= playerStepSize;
  break;
case Movement.Right:
  x += playerStepSize;
  break;
case Movement.Top:
  y += playerStepSize;
  break;
case Movement.Bottom:
  y -= playerStepSize;
  break;
}
```

If the user was not aligned on the grid, we do not have to check whether the player collides with a wall. Otherwise, we must validate it. If the user then does collide with a wall, we return the old player with the old location:

```
if (onGrid(player) && collidesWall(x, y, walls)) {
  return player;
}
return { x, y };
}
```

We can filter the dots by calculating the distance to Pac Man. When they are close to the player, they are eaten by Pac Man and filtered out:

```
function stepDots(dots: Object[], player: Object) {
  return dots.filter(dot => distance(dot.x, dot.y, player.x, player.y) >=
0.55)
}
```

The time handler can now update the state: the player moves, the enemies try to move toward the player, and the player can eat dots.

Running the game

To start the game, we must call the game function with the default state, draw function, time handler, and event handler. In lib/game/index.ts, we write the following code to start the game:

```
import { game } from "../framework/game";
import { defaultState } from "./model";
import { draw } from "./view";
import { step } from "./step";
import { eventHandler } from "./event";

const canvas = <HTMLCanvasElement> document.getElementById("game");
game(canvas, document.body, 60, defaultState, draw, step, eventHandler);
```

We can compile the game by executing gulp. You can play the game by opening static/index.html.

As you will see, nothing happens when you have eaten all of the dots, or when you get hit by an enemy. In the next section, we will implement a menu. When the player wins or loses, we will show this menu.

Adding a menu

To finish off the game, we will add some menus to it. In the main menu, the user can choose a difficulty. The user can select an option using the arrow keys and confirm using the spacebar. The menu will look like this:

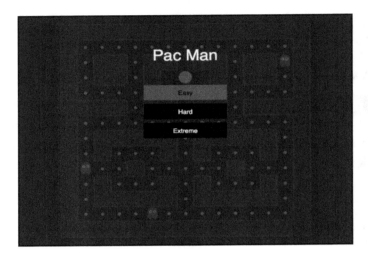

To implement the menu, we must add it to the state. Then we can render the menu and update the menu state in the event handler. We start by updating the state.

Changing the model

In `lib/game/model.ts`, we will add the menus to the state. First, we will create a new type for the menu. The menu contains a title, a list of options, and the index of the selected button. Each option has a string and a function that applies the action by transforming the state:

```
export interface Menu {
  title: string;
  options: [string, (state: State) => State][];
  selected: number;
}
```

We add the `menu` to the `State`:

```
export interface State {
  menu: Menu | undefined;
  level: Level;
}
```

The main menu will contain three buttons; to start an easy, hard, or extreme game. We will define a function that can start the game with a specified difficulty:

```
const startGame = (difficulty: Difficulty) => (state: State) => ({
  menu: undefined,
  level: update(defaultLevel, { difficulty })
});
```

Now we can define the main menu:

```
export const menuMain: Menu = {
  title: "Pac Man",
  options: [
    ["Easy", startGame(Difficulty.Easy)],
    ["Hard", startGame(Difficulty.Hard)],
    ["Extreme", startGame(Difficulty.Extreme)]
  ],
  selected: 0
}
```

We can define two more menus, which are shown when the user wins or dies:

```
export const menuWon: Menu = {
  title: "You won!",
  options: [
    ["Back", state => ({ menu: menuMain, level: state.level })]
  ],
  selected: 0
}
export const menuLost: Menu = {
  title: "Game over!",
  options: [
    ["Back", state => ({ menu: menuMain, level: state.level })]
  ],
  selected: 0
}
```

We can use this menu in the starting state of the application:

```
export const defaultState: State = {
  menu: menuMain,
  level: defaultLevel
};
```

Since the menu is a part of the default state, the game will start with the menu. In the next sections, we will render the menu and handle its events.

Rendering the menu

We must update lib/game/view.ts to draw the menu on the canvas. We change the draw function:

```
export function draw(state: State, width: number, height: number) {
  return new Pictures([
    drawLevel(state.level, width, height),
    drawMenu(state.menu, width, height)
  ]);
}
```

Next, we create drawMenu, that will render the level. It will show the title and the buttons. The selected button gets a different color:

```
function drawMenu(menu: Menu | undefined, width: number, height: number):
Picture {
    if (menu === undefined) return new Empty();
    const selected = menu.selected;
    const background = new Color("rgba(40,40,40,0.8)", new
    Rectangle(0, 0, width, height));
    const title = new Translate(0, 200, new Scale(4, 4,
        new Color("#fff", new Text(menu.title, font))
    ));
    const options = new Pictures(menu.options.map(showOption));

    return new Pictures([background, title, options]);

    function showOption(item: [string, (state: State) => State],
    index: number) {
        const isSelected = index === selected;
        return new Translate(0, 100 - index * 50, new Pictures([
            new Color(isSelected ? "#ff0000" : "#000000",
                new Rectangle(0, 0, 200, 40)),
            new Color(isSelected ? "#000000" : "#ffffff",
                new Scale(1.6, 1.6, new Text(item[0], font)))
```

```
        ]));
    }
}
```

This function will now draw the menu when it is active. We must still handle the events of the menu. We will do that in the next section.

Handling events

In `lib/game/event.ts`, we will handle the events for the menu. We must update the index of the selected item when the user presses the up or down key. When the user presses space, we execute the action of the selected button. First, we must adjust `eventHandler` to call `eventHandlerMenu` when the menu is visible.

```
export function eventHandler(state: State, event: KeyEvent) {
  if (state.menu) {
    return eventHandlerMenu(state, event);
  } else {
    return eventHandlerPlaying(state, event);
  }
}
```

Next, we create `eventHandlerMenu`.

```
function eventHandlerMenu(state: State, event: KeyEvent) {

    if (event instanceof KeyEvent && event.kind === KeyEventKind.Press) {
        const menu = state.menu!;
        let selected = menu.selected;
        switch (event.keyCode) {
            case Keys.Top:
                selected--;
                if (selected < 0) {
                    selected = menu.options.length - 1;
                }
                return {
                    menu: update(menu, {
                        selected
                    }),
                    level: state.level
                };
            case Keys.Bottom:
                selected++;
                if (selected >= menu.options.length) {
                    selected = 0;
                }
```

```
                        return {
                            menu: update(menu, {
                                selected
                            }),
                            level: state.level
                        };
                    case Keys.Space:
                        const option = menu.options[menu.selected];
                        return option[1](state);
                    default:
                        return state;
                }
            }
        return state;
    }
```

You can navigate through the menu using the arrow keys and the space bar. However, in the background, the game is still running. In the next section, we will not update the state of the level when the menu is active. Also, we will show a menu when the user has won or lost.

Modifying the time handler

In lib/game/step.ts, we must show the menu when the user won or lost. We must change the import-statement to import menuLost and menuWon from model:

```
import { State, Level, Object, Enemy, Wall, Movement, isOppositeMovement,
menuLost, menuWon, onGrid, Difficulty } from "./model";
```

In newMenu, we check whether such a menu should be shown.

```
function newMenu(player: Object, dots: Object[], enemies: Enemy[]) {
  for (const enemy of enemies) {
    if (distance(enemy.x, enemy.y, player.x, player.y) <= 1) {
      return menuLost;
    }
  }
  if (dots.length === 0) return menuWon;
  return undefined;
}
```

In stepLevel, we must call this function.

```
function stepLevel(state: State): State {
  const level = state.level;
  const enemies = level.enemies.map(enemy => stepEnemy(enemy, level.player,
```

```
level.walls, level.difficulty));
  const player = stepPlayer(level.player, level.currentMovement,
level.walls);
  const dots = stepDots(level.dots, player);
  const currentMovement = onGrid(player) ||
isOppositeMovement(level.inputMovement, level.currentMovement) ?
level.inputMovement : level.currentMovement;
  const menu = newMenu(player, dots, enemies);
  const newLevel = update(level, { enemies, dots, player, currentMovement
});
  return update(state, { level: newLevel, menu });
}
```

Finally, we must not call `stepLevel` in `step` if the menu is active.

```
export function step(state: State) {
  if (state.menu === undefined) {
    return stepLevel(state);
  } else {
    return state;
  }
}
```

We can now compile the game again with `gulp` and run it by opening `static/index.html`.

Summary

In this chapter, we have explored the HTML canvas. We have seen how we can design a framework to use functional programming. The framework provides abstraction around drawing on the canvas, which is not pure.

We have built the game Pac Man. The structure of this application was similar to a Flux architecture, like we saw in the previous chapter.

The enemies in this game are not very smart. They easily get stuck behind a wall. In the next chapter, we will take a look at another game, but we will only focus on the artificial intelligence (AI). We will create an application that can play Tic-Tac-Toe without losing. We will see how a Minimax strategy works and how we can implement it in TypeScript.

9
Playing Tic-Tac-Toe against an AI

We built the game Pac Man in the previous chapter. The enemies were not very smart; you can easily fool them. In this chapter, we will build a game in which the computer will play well. The game is called **Tic-Tac-Toe**. The game is played by two players on a grid, usually three by three. The players try to place their symbols three in a row (horizontal, vertical or diagonal). The first player can place crosses, the second player places circles. If the board is full, and no one has three symbols in a row, it is a draw.

The game is usually played on a three-by-three grid and the target is to have three symbols in a row. To make the application more interesting, we will make the dimension and the row length variable.

We will not create a graphical interface for this application, since we have already done that in `Chapter 6`, *Advanced Programming in TypeScript*. We will only build the game mechanics and the **artificial intelligence** (**AI**). An AI is a player controlled by the computer. If implemented correctly, the computer should never lose on a standard three by three grid. When the computer plays against the computer, it will result in a draft. We will also write various unit tests for the application.

We will build the game as a command-line application. That means you can play the game in a terminal. You can interact with the game only with text input:

```
It's player one's turn!
Choose one out of these options:
1    X|X|
     -+-+-
      |O|
     -+-+-
      | |
```

```
2    X|  |X
     -+-+-
      |O|
     -+-+-
      |  |
3    X|  |
     -+-+-
     X|O|
     -+-+-
      |  |
4    X|  |
     -+-+-
      |O|X
     -+-+-
      |  |
5    X|  |
     -+-+-
      |O|
     -+-+-
     X|  |
6    X|  |
     -+-+-
      |O|
     -+-+-
      |X|
7    X|  |
     -+-+-
      |O|
     -+-+-
      |  |X
```

We will build this application in the following steps:

- Creating the project structure
- Adding utility functions
- Creating the models
- Implementing the AI using Minimax
- Creating the interface
- Testing the AI
- Summary

Creating the project structure

We will locate the source files in `lib` and the tests in `lib/test`. We use `gulp` to compile the project and **AVA** to run tests. We can install the dependencies of our project with NPM:

```
npm init -y
npm install ava gulp gulp-typescript --save-dev
```

In `gulpfile.js`, we configure `gulp` to compile our TypeScript files:

```
var gulp = require("gulp");
var ts = require("gulp-typescript");

var tsProject = ts.createProject("./lib/tsconfig.json");

gulp.task("default", function() {
  return tsProject.src()
    .pipe(ts(tsProject))
    .pipe(gulp.dest("dist"));
});
```

Configure TypeScript

We can download type definitions for NodeJS with NPM:

```
npm install @types/node --save-dev
```

We must exclude browser files in TypeScript. In `lib/tsconfig.json`, we add the configuration for TypeScript:

```
{
  "compilerOptions": {
    "target": "es6",
    "module": "commonjs"
  }
}
```

For applications that run in the browser, you will probably want to target ES5, since ES6 is not supported in all browsers. However, this application will only be executed in NodeJS, so we do not have such limitations. You have to use NodeJS 6 or later for ES6 support.

Adding utility functions

Since we will work a lot with arrays, we can use some utility functions. First, we create a function that flattens a two dimensional array into a one dimensional array:

```
export function flatten<U>(array: U[][]) {
  return (<U[]>[]).concat(...array);
}
```

Next, we create a `function` that replaces a single element of an `array` with a specified value. We will use functional programming in this chapter again, so we must use immutable data structures. We can use map for this, since this function provides both the element and the index to the callback. With this `index`, we can determine whether that element should be replaced:

```
export function arrayModify<U>(array: U[], index: number, newValue: U) {
  return array.map((oldValue, currentIndex) =>
    currentIndex === index ? newValue : oldValue);
}
```

We also create a function that returns a random integer under a certain upper bound:

```
export function randomInt(max: number) {
  return Math.floor(Math.random() * max);
}
```

We will use these functions in the next sessions.

Creating the models

In `lib/model.ts`, we will create the model for our game. The model should contain the game state.

We start with the player. The game is played by two players. Each field of the grid contains the symbol of a player or no symbol. We will model the grid as a two dimensional array, where each field can contain a player:

```
export type Grid = Player[][];
```

A player is either `Player1`, `Player2`, or no player:

```
export enum Player {
  Player1 = 1,
  Player2 = -1,
```

```
    None = 0
}
```

We have given these members values so we can easily get the opponent of a player:

```
export function getOpponent(player: Player): Player {
  return -player;
}
```

We create a type to represent an index of the grid. Since the grid is two dimensional, such an index requires two values:

```
export type Index = [number, number];
```

We can use this type to create two functions that get or update one field of the grid. We use functional programming in this chapter, so we will not modify the grid. Instead, we return a new grid with one field changed:

```
export function get(grid: Grid, [rowIndex, columnIndex]: Index) {
  const row = grid[rowIndex];
  if (!row) return undefined;
  return row[columnIndex];
}
export function set(grid: Grid, [row, column]: Index, value: Player) {
  return arrayModify(grid, row,
    arrayModify(grid[row], column, value)
  );
}
```

Showing the grid

To show the game to the user, we must convert a grid to a string. First, we will create a function that converts a player to a string, then a function that uses the previous function to show a row, finally a function that uses these functions to show the complete grid.

The string representation of a grid should have lines between the fields. We create these lines with standard characters (+, −, and |). This gives the following result:

```
X|X|O
-+-+-
 |O|
-+-+-
X| |
```

To convert a player to the string, we must get their symbol. For `Player1`, that is a cross and for `Player2`, a circle. If a field of the grid contains no symbol, we return a space to keep the grid aligned:

```
function showPlayer(player: Player) {
  switch (player) {
    case Player.Player1:
      return "X";
    case Player.Player2:
      return "O";
    default:
      return " ";
  }
}
```

We can use this function to the tokens of all fields in a row. We add a separator between these fields:

```
function showRow(row: Player[]) {
  return row.map(showPlayer).reduce((previous, current) => previous + "|" +
current);
}
```

Since we must do the same later on, but with a different separator, we create a small helper function that does this concatenation based on a separator:

```
const concat = (separator: string) => (left: string, right: string) =>
  left + separator + right;
```

This function requires the separator and returns a function that can be passed to reduce. We can now use this function in `showRow`:

```
function showRow(row: Player[]) {
  return row.map(showPlayer).reduce(concat("|"));
}
```

We can also use this helper function to show the entire grid. First we must compose the separator, which is almost the same as showing a single row. Next, we can show the grid with this separator:

```
export function showGrid(grid: Grid) {
  const separator = "\n" + grid[0].map(() => "-").reduce(concat("+")) +
"\n";
  return grid.map(showRow).reduce(concat(separator));
}
```

Creating operations on the grid

We will now create some functions that do operations on the grid. These functions check whether the board is full, whether someone has won, and what options a player has.

We can check whether the board is full by looking at all fields. If no field exists that has no symbol on it, the board is full, as every field has a symbol:

```
export function isFull(grid: Grid) {
  for (const row of grid) {
    for (const field of row) {
      if (field === Player.None) return false;
    }
  }
  return true;
}
```

To check whether a user has won, we must get a list of all horizontal, vertical and diagonal rows. For each row, we can check whether a row consists of a certain amount of the same symbols on a row. We store the grid as an array of the horizontal rows, so we can easily get those rows. We can also get the vertical rows relatively easily:

```
function allRows(grid: Grid) {
  return [
    ...grid,
    ...grid[0].map((field, index) => getVertical(index)),
    ...
  ];
  function getVertical(index: number) {
    return grid.map(row => row[index]);
  }
}
```

Getting a diagonal row requires some more work. We create a helper function that will walk on the `grid` from a start point, in a certain direction. We distinguish two different kinds of diagonals: a diagonal that goes to the lower-right and a diagonal that goes to the lower-left.

For a standard three by three game, only two diagonals exist. However, a larger grid may have more diagonals. If the grid is 5 by 5, and the users should get three in a row, ten diagonals with a length of at least three exist:

1. 0, 0 to 4, 4
2. 0, 1 to 3, 4
3. 0, 2 to 2, 4

4. 1, 0 to 4, 3
5. 2, 0 to 4, 2
6. 4, 0 to 0, 4
7. 3, 0 to 0, 3
8. 2, 0 to 0, 2
9. 4, 1 to 1, 4
10. 4, 2 to 2, 4

The diagonals that go toward the lower-right, start at the first column or at the first horizontal row. Other diagonals start at the last column or at the first horizontal row. In this function, we will just return all diagonals, even if they only have one element, since that is easy to implement.

We implement this with a function that walks the grid to find the diagonal. That function requires a start position and a `step` function. The `step` function increments the position for a specific direction:

```
function allRows(grid: Grid) {
  return [
    ...grid,
    ...grid[0].map((field, index) => getVertical(index)),
    ...grid.map((row, index) => getDiagonal([index, 0], stepDownRight)),
    ...grid[0].slice(1).map((field, index) => getDiagonal([0, index + 1],
stepDownRight)),
    ...grid.map((row, index) => getDiagonal([index, grid[0].length - 1],
stepDownLeft)),
    ...grid[0].slice(1).map((field, index) => getDiagonal([0, index],
stepDownLeft))
  ];
  function getVertical(index: number) {
    return grid.map(row => row[index]);
  }
  function getDiagonal(start: Index, step: (index: Index) =>
Index) {
      const row: Player[] = [];
      let index: Index | undefined = start;
      let value = get(grid, index);
      while (value !== undefined) {
          row.push(value);
          index = step(index);
          value = get(grid, index);
      }
      return row;
  }
  function stepDownRight([i, j]: Index): Index {
```

```
      return [i + 1, j + 1];
    }
    function stepDownLeft([i, j]: Index): Index {  .
      return [i + 1, j - 1];
    }
    function stepUpRight([i, j]: Index): Index {
      return [i - 1, j + 1];
    }
  }
```

To check whether a row has a certain amount of the same elements on a row, we will create a function with some nice looking functional programming. The function requires the array, the player, and the index at which the checking starts. That index will usually be zero, but during recursion we can set it to a different value. `originalLength` contains the original length that a sequence should have. The last parameter, `length`, will have the same value in most cases, but in recursion we will change the value. We start with some base cases. Every row contains a sequence of zero symbols, so we can always return `true` in such a case:

```
    function isWinningRow(row: Player[], player: Player, index: number,
    originalLength: number, length: number): boolean {
      if (length === 0) {
        return true;
      }
```

If the row does not contain enough elements to form a sequence, the row will not have such a sequence and we can return `false`:

```
      if (index + length > row.length) {
        return false;
      }
```

For other cases, we use recursion. If the current element contains a symbol of the provided player, this row forms a sequence if the next length-1 fields contain the same symbol:

```
      if (row[index] === player) {
        return isWinningRow(row, player, index + 1, originalLength, length -
    1);
      }
```

Otherwise, the row should contain a sequence of the original length in some other position:

```
      return isWinningRow(row, player, index + 1, originalLength,
    originalLength);
    }
```

If the grid is large enough, a row could contain a long enough sequence after a sequence that was too short. For instance, XXOXXX contains a sequence of length three. This function handles these rows correctly with the parameters originalLength and length.

Finally, we must create a function that returns all possible sets that a player can do. To implement this function, we must first find all indices. We filter these indices to indices that reference an empty field. For each of these indices, we change the value of the grid into the specified player. This results in a list of options for the player:

```
export function getOptions(grid: Grid, player: Player) {
  const rowIndices = grid.map((row, index) => index);
  const columnIndices = grid[0].map((column, index) => index);
  const allFields = flatten(rowIndices.map(
    row => columnIndices.map(column => <Index> [row, column])
  ));
  return allFields
    .filter(index => get(grid, index) === Player.None)
    .map(index => set(grid, index, player));
}
```

The AI will use this to choose the best option and a human player will get a menu with these options.

Creating the grid

Before the game can be started, we must create an empty grid. We will write a function that creates an empty grid with the specified size:

```
export function createGrid(width: number, height: number) {
  const grid: Grid = [];
  for (let i = 0; i < height; i++) {
    grid[i] = [];
    for (let j = 0; j < width; j++) {
      grid[i][j] = Player.None;
    }
  }
  return grid;
}
```

In the next section, we will add some tests for the functions that we have written. These functions work on the grid, so it will be useful to have a function that can parse a grid based on a string.

We will separate the rows of a grid with a semicolon. Each row contains tokens for each field. For instance, "XXO; O ;X " results in this grid:

```
X|X|O
-+-+-
 |O|
-+-+-
X| |
```

We can implement this by splitting the string into an array of lines. For each line, we split
the line into an array of characters. We map these characters to a Player value:

```
export function parseGrid(input: string) {
  const lines = input.split(";");
  return lines.map(parseLine);
  function parseLine(line: string) {
    return line.split("").map(parsePlayer);
  }
  function parsePlayer(character: string) {
    switch (character) {
      case "X":
        return Player.Player1;
      case "O":
        return Player.Player2;
      default:
        return Player.None;
    }
  }
}
```

In the next section we will use this function to write some tests.

Adding tests

Just like in Chapter 5, *Native QR Scanner App*, we will use AVA to write tests for our
application. Since the functions do not have side effects, we can easily test them.

In lib/test/winner.ts, we test the findWinner function. First, we check whether the
function recognizes the winner in some simple cases:

```
import test from "ava";
import { Player, parseGrid, findWinner } from "../model";

test("player winner", t => {
  t.is(findWinner(parseGrid("   ;XXX;   "), 3), Player.Player1);
  t.is(findWinner(parseGrid("   ;OOO;   "), 3), Player.Player2);
  t.is(findWinner(parseGrid("   ;   ;   "), 3), Player.None);
});
```

We can also test all possible three-in-a-row positions in the three by three grid. With this test, we can find out whether horizontal, vertical, and diagonal rows are checked correctly:

```
test ("3x3 winner", t => {
  const grids = [
    "XXX;    ;    ",
    "   ;XXX;    ",
    "   ;    ;XXX",
    "X  ;X  ;X  ",
    " X ; X ; X ",
    "  X;  X;  X",
    "X  ; X ;  X",
    "  X; X ;X  "
  ];
  for (const grid of grids) {
    t.is (findWinner (parseGrid (grid), 3), Player.Player1);
  }
});
```

We must also test that the function does not claim that someone won too often. In the next test, we validate that the function does not return a winner for grids that do not have a winner:

```
test ("3x3 no winner", t => {
  const grids = [
    "XXO;OXX;XOO",
    "   ;    ;    ",
    "XXO;    ;OOX",
    "X  ;X  ; X "
  ];
  for (const grid of grids) {
    t.is (findWinner (parseGrid (grid), 3), Player.None);
  }
});
```

Since the game also supports other dimensions, we should check these too. We check that all diagonals of a four by three grid are checked correctly, where the length of a sequence should be two:

```
test ("4x3 winner", t => {
  const grids = [
    "X  ; X ;    ",
    " X ;  X ;    ",
    "  X ;   X;    ",
    "   ;X  ; X ",
    "  X ;   X;    ",
    " X ;  X ;    ",
    "X  ; X ;    ",
```

```
    "   ;   X;   X  "
  ];
  for (const grid of grids) {
    t.is(findWinner(parseGrid(grid), 2), Player.Player1);
  }
});
```

You can of course add more test grids yourself.

 Add tests before you fix a bug. These tests should show the wrong behavior related to the bug. When you have fixed the bug, these tests should pass. This prevents the bug returning in a future version.

Random testing

Instead of running the test on some predefined set of test cases, you can also write tests that run on random data. You cannot compare the output of a function directly with an expected value, but you can check some properties of it. For instance, getOptions should return an empty list if and only if the board is full. We can use this property to test getOptions and isFull.

First, we create a function that randomly chooses a player. To higher the chance of a full grid, we add some extra weight on the players compared to an empty field:

```
import test from "ava";
import { createGrid, Player, isFull, getOptions } from "../model";
import { randomInt } from "../utils";

function randomPlayer() {
  switch (randomInt(4)) {
    case 0:
    case 1:
      return Player.Player1;
    case 2:
    case 3:
      return Player.Player2;
    default:
      return Player.None;
  }
}
```

We create 10000 random grids with this function. The dimensions and the fields are chosen randomly:

```
test("get-options", t => {
   for (let i = 0; i < 10000; i++) {
      const grid = createGrid(randomInt(10) + 1, randomInt(10) + 1)
         .map(row => row.map(randomPlayer));
```

Next, we check whether the property that we describe holds for this grid:

```
      const options = getOptions(grid, Player.Player1)
      t.is(isFull(grid), options.length === 0);
```

We also check that the function does not give the same option twice:

```
      for (let i = 1; i < options.length; i++) {
         for (let j = 0; j < i; j++) {
            t.notSame(options[i], options[j]);
         }
      }
   }
});
```

Depending on how critical a function is, you can add more tests. In this case, you could check that only one field is modified in an option or that only an empty field can be modified in an option:

Now you can run the tests using `gulp && ava dist/test`. You can add this to your `package.json` file. In the scripts section, you can add commands that you want to run. With `npm run xxx`, you can run task `xxx`. `npm test` that was added as shorthand for `npm run test`, since the test command is often used:

```
{
  "name": "chapter-7",
  "version": "1.0.0",
  "scripts": {
  "test": "gulp && ava dist/test"
  },
  ...
```

Implementing the AI using Minimax

We create an AI based on **Minimax**. The computer cannot know what his opponent will do in the next steps, but he can check what he can do in the worst-case. The minimum outcome of these worst cases is maximized by this algorithm. This behavior has given Minimax its name.

To learn how Minimax works, we will take a look at the value or score of a grid. If the game is finished, we can easily define its value: if you won, the value is 1; if you lost, -1 and if it is a draw, 0. Thus, for player 1 the next grid has value 1 and for player 2 the value is -1:

```
X|X|X
-+-+-
O|O|
-+-+-
X|O|
```

We will also define the value of a grid for a game that has not been finished. We take a look at the following grid:

```
X| |X
-+-+-
O|O|
-+-+-
O|X|
```

It is player 1's turn. He can place his stone on the top row, and he would win, resulting in a value of 1. He can also choose to lay his stone on the second row. Then the game will result in a draft, if player 2 is not dumb, with score 0. If he chooses to place the stone on the last row, player 2 can win resulting in -1. We assume that player 1 is smart and that he will go for the first option. Thus, we could say that the value of this unfinished game is 1.

We will now formalize this. In the previous paragraph, we have summed up all options for the player. For each option, we have calculated the minimum value that the player could get if he would choose that option. From these options, we have chosen the maximum value.

Minimax chooses the option with the highest value of all options.

Implementing Minimax in TypeScript

As you can see, the definition of Minimax looks like you can implement it with recursion. We create a function that returns both the best option and the value of the game. A function can only return a single value, but multiple values can be combined into a single value in a tuple, which is an array with these values.

First, we handle the base cases. If the game is finished, the player has no options and the value can be calculated directly:

```
import { Player, Grid, findWinner, isFull, getOpponent, getOptions } from
"./model";

export function minimax(grid: Grid, rowLength: number, player: Player):
[Grid, number] {
  const winner = findWinner(grid, rowLength);
  if (winner === player) {
    return [undefined, 1];
  } else if (winner !== Player.None) {
    return [undefined, -1];
  } else if (isFull(grid)) {
    return [undefined, 0];
```

Otherwise, we list all options. For all options, we calculate the value. The value of an option is the same as the opposite of the value of the option for the opponent. Finally, we choose the option with the best value:

```
  } else {
    let options = getOptions(grid, player);
    const opponent = getOpponent(player);
    return options.map<[Grid, number]>(
      option => [option, -(minimax(option, rowLength, opponent)[1])]
    ).reduce(
      (previous, current) => previous[1] < current[1] ? current : previous
    )!;
  }
}
```

When you use tuple types, you should explicitly add a type definition for it. Since tuples are arrays too, an array type is automatically inferred. When you add the tuple as return type, expressions after the return keyword will be inferred as these tuples. For options.map, you can mention the union type as a type argument or by specifying it in the callback function (`options.map((option): [Grid, number] => ...);`).

You can easily see that such an AI can also be used for other kinds of games. Actually, the `minimax` function has no direct reference to Tic-Tac-Toe, only `findWinner`, `isFull` and `getOptions` are related to Tic-Tac-Toe.

Optimizing the algorithm

The Minimax algorithm can be slow. Choosing the first set, especially, takes a long time since the algorithm tries all ways of playing the game. We will use two techniques to speed up the algorithm.

First, we can use the symmetry of the game. When the board is empty it does not matter whether you place a stone in the upper-left corner or the lower-right corner. Rotating the grid around the center 180 degrees gives an equivalent board. Thus, we only need to take a look at half the options when the board is empty.

Secondly, we can stop searching for options if we found an option with value 1. Such an option is already the best thing to do.

Implementing these techniques gives the following function:

```
import { Player, Grid, findWinner, isFull, getOpponent, getOptions } from
"./model";

export function minimax(grid: Grid, rowLength: number, player: Player):
[Grid, number] {
  const winner = findWinner(grid, rowLength);
  if (winner === player) {
    return [undefined, 1];
  } else if (winner !== Player.None) {
    return [undefined, -1];
  } else if (isFull(grid)) {
    return [undefined, 0];
  } else {
    let options = getOptions(grid, player);
    const gridSize = grid.length * grid[0].length;
    if (options.length === gridSize) {
      options = options.slice(0, Math.ceil(gridSize / 2));
    }
    const opponent = getOpponent(player);
    let best: [Grid, number] | undefined = undefined;
    for (const option of options) {
      const current: [Grid, number] = [option, -(minimax(option, rowLength,
opponent)[1])];
      if (current[1] === 1) {
        return current;
```

```
        } else if (best === undefined || current[1] > best[1]) {
          best = current;
        }
      }
    }
    return best!;
  }
}
```

This will speed up the AI. In the next sections we will implement the interface for the game and we will write some tests for the AI.

Creating the interface

NodeJS can be used to create servers, as we did in chapters 2 and 3. You can also create tools with a **command line interface (CLI).** For instance, gulp, NPM and typings are command line interfaces built with NodeJS. We will use NodeJS to create the interface for our game.

Handling interaction

The interaction from the user can only happen by text input in the terminal. When the game starts, it will ask the user some questions about the configuration: width, height, row length for a sequence, and the player(s) that are played by the computer. The highlighted lines are the input of the user:

```
Tic-Tac-Toe

Width
3
Height
3
Row length
2
Who controls player 1?
1   You

2   Computer

1
Who controls player 2?
1   You

2   Computer
```

1

During the game, the game asks the user which of the possible options he wants to do. All possible steps are shown on the screen, with an index. The user can type the index of the option he wants:

```
X| |
-+-+-
O|O|
-+-+-
 |X|
It's player one's turn!
Choose one out of these options:
1  X|X|
   -+-+-
   O|O|
   -+-+-
    |X|
2  X| |X
   -+-+-
   O|O|
   -+-+-
    |X|
3  X| |
   -+-+-
   O|O|X
   -+-+-
    |X|
4  X| |
   -+-+-
   O|O|
   -+-+-
   X|X|
5  X| |
   -+-+-
   O|O|
   -+-+-
    |X|X
```

A NodeJS application has three standard streams to interact with the user. Standard input, **stdin**, is used to receive input from the user. Standard output, **stdout**, is used to show text to the user. Standard error, **stderr**, is used to show error messages to the user. You can access these streams with `process.stdin`, `process.stdout` and `process.stderr`.

You have probably already used `console.log` to write text to the console. This function writes the text to `stdout`. We will use `console.log` to write text to `stdout` and we will not use `stderr`.

We will create a helper function that reads a line from `stdin`. This is an asynchronous task, the function starts listening and resolves when the user hits enter. In `lib/cli.ts`, we start by importing the types and function that we have written.

```
import { Grid, Player, getOptions, getOpponent, showGrid, findWinner,
isFull, createGrid } from "./model";
import { minimax } from "./ai";
```

We can listen to input from stdin using the `data` event. The process sends either the string or a buffer, an efficient way to store binary data in memory. With `once`, the callback will only be fired once. If you want to listen to all occurrences of the event, you can use `on`:

```
function readLine() {
  return new Promise<string>(resolve => {
    process.stdin.once("data", (data: string | Buffer) =>
resolve(data.toString())));
  });
}
```

We can easily use `readLine` in async functions. For instance, we can now create a function that reads, parses and validates a line. We can use this to read the input of the user, parse it to a number, and finally check that the number is within a certain range. This function will return the value if it passes the validator. Otherwise it shows a message and retries.

```
async function readAndValidate<U>(message: string, parse: (data: string) =>
U, validate: (value: U) => boolean): Promise<U> {
  const data = await readLine();
  const value = parse(data);
  if (validate(value)) {
    return value;
  } else {
    console.log(message);
    return readAndValidate(message, parse, validate);
  }
}
```

We can use this function to show a question where the user has various options. The user should type the index of his answer. This function validates that the index is within bounds. We will show indices starting at 1 to the user, so we must carefully handle these.

```
async function choose(question: string, options: string[]) {
  console.log(question);
  for (let i = 0; i < options.length; i++) {
    console.log((i + 1) + "\t" + options[i].replace(/\n/g, "\n\t"));
    console.log();
  }
  return await readAndValidate(
```

```
    `Enter a number between 1 and ${ options.length }`,
    parseInt,
    index => index >= 1 && index <= options.length
  ) - 1;
}
```

Creating players

A player could either be a human or the computer. We create a type that can contain both kinds of players.

```
type PlayerController = (grid: Grid) => Grid | Promise<Grid>;
```

Next we create a function that creates such a player. For a user, we must first know whether he is the first or the second player. Then we return an async function that asks the player which step he wants to do.

```
const getUserPlayer = (player: Player) => async (grid: Grid) => {
  const options = getOptions(grid, player);
  const index = await choose("Choose one out of these options:",
options.map(showGrid));
  return options[index];
};
```

For the AI player, we must know the player index and the length of a sequence. We use these variables and the grid of the game to run the Minimax algorithm.

```
const getAIPlayer = (player: Player, rowLength: number) => (grid: Grid) =>
    minimax(grid, rowLength, player)[0]!;
```

Now we can create a function that asks the player whether a player should be played by the user or the computer.

```
async function getPlayer(index: number, player: Player, rowLength: number):
Promise<PlayerController> {
  switch (await choose(`Who controls player ${ index }?`, ["You",
"Computer"])) {
    case 0:
      return getUserPlayer(player);
    default:
      return getAIPlayer(player, rowLength);
  }
}
```

We combine these functions in a function that handles the whole game. First, we must ask the user to provide the width, height and length of a sequence.

```
export async function game() {
  console.log("Tic-Tac-Toe");
  console.log();
  console.log("Width");
  const width = await readAndValidate("Enter an integer", parseInt,
isFinite);
  console.log("Height");
  const height = await readAndValidate("Enter an integer", parseInt,
isFinite);
  console.log("Row length");
  const rowLength = await readAndValidate("Enter an integer", parseInt,
isFinite);
```

We ask the user which players should be controlled by the computer.

```
  const player1 = await getPlayer(1, Player.Player1, rowLength);
  const player2 = await getPlayer(2, Player.Player2, rowLength);
```

The user can now play the game. We do not use a loop, but we use recursion to give the player their turns.

```
  return play(createGrid(width, height), Player.Player1);
  async function play(grid: Grid, player: Player): Promise<[Grid, Player]>
  {
```

In every step, we show the grid. If the game is finished, we show which player has won.

```
    console.log();
    console.log(showGrid(grid));
    console.log();
    const winner = findWinner(grid, rowLength);
    if (winner === Player.Player1) {
      console.log("Player 1 has won!");
      return <[Grid, Player]> [grid, winner];
    } else if (winner === Player.Player2) {
      console.log("Player 2 has won!");
      return <[Grid, Player]>[grid, winner];
    } else if (isFull(grid)) {
      console.log("It's a draw!");
      return <[Grid, Player]>[grid, Player.None];
    }
```

If the game is not finished, we ask the current player or the computer which set he wants to do.

```
    console.log(`It's player ${ player === Player.Player1 ? "one's" :
"two's" } turn!`);
    const current = player === Player.Player1 ? player1 : player2;
    return play(await current(grid), getOpponent(player));
  }
}
```

In `lib/index.ts`, we can start the game. When the game is finished, we must manually exit the process.

```
import { game } from "./cli";

game().then(() => process.exit());
```

We can compile and run this in a terminal:

```
gulp && node --harmony_destructuring dist
```

At the time of writing, NodeJS requires the `--harmony_destructuring` flag to allow destructuring, like `[x, y] = z`. In future versions of NodeJS, this flag will be removed and you can run it without it.

Testing the AI

We will add some tests to check that the AI works properly. For a standard three by three game, the AI should never lose. That means when an AI plays against an AI, it should result in a draw. We can add a test for this. In `lib/test/ai.ts`, we import AVA and our own definitions.

```
import test from "ava";
import { createGrid, Grid, findWinner, isFull, getOptions, Player } from
"../model";
import { minimax } from "../ai";
import { randomInt } from "../utils";
```

We create a function that simulates the whole gameplay.

```
type PlayerController = (grid: Grid) => Grid;
function run(grid: Grid, a: PlayerController, b: PlayerController): Player
{
  const winner = findWinner(grid, 3);
  if (winner !== Player.None) return winner;
```

```
   if (isFull(grid)) return Player.None;
   return run(a(grid), b, a);
}
```

We write a function that executes a step for the AI.

```
const aiPlayer = (player: Player) => (grid: Grid) =>
   minimax(grid, 3, player)[0]!;
```

Now we create the test that validates that a game where the AI plays against the AI results in a draw.

```
test("AI vs AI", t => {
   const result = run(createGrid(3, 3), aiPlayer(Player.Player1),
aiPlayer(Player.Player2))
   t.is(result, Player.None);
});
```

Testing with a random player

We can also test what happens when the AI plays against a random player or when a player plays against the AI. The AI should win or it should result in a draw. We run these multiple times; what you should always do when you use randomization in your test.

We create a function that creates the random player.

```
const randomPlayer = (player: Player) => (grid: Grid) => {
   const options = getOptions(grid, player);
   return options[randomInt(options.length)];
};
```

We write the two tests that both run 20 games with a random player and an AI.

```
test("random vs AI", t => {
   for (let i = 0; i < 20; i++) {
      const result = run(createGrid(3, 3), randomPlayer(Player.Player1),
aiPlayer(Player.Player2))
      t.not(result, Player.Player1);
   }
});

test("AI vs random", t => {
   for (let i = 0; i < 20; i++) {
      const result = run(createGrid(3, 3), aiPlayer(Player.Player1),
randomPlayer(Player.Player2))
      t.not(result, Player.Player2);
```

```
    }
});
```

We have written different kinds of tests:

- Tests that check the exact results of single function
- Tests that check a certain property of results of a function
- Tests that check a big component

Always start writing tests for small components. If the AI tests should fail, that could be caused by a mistake in `hasWinner`, `isFull` or `getOptions`, so it is hard to find the location of the error. Only testing small components is not enough; bigger tests, such as the AI tests, are closer to what the user will do. Bigger tests are harder to create, especially when you want to test the user interface. You must also not forget that tests cannot guarantee that your code runs correctly, it just guarantees that your test cases work correctly.

Summary

In this chapter, we have written an AI for Tic-Tac-Toe. With the command line interface, you can play this game against the AI or another human. You can also see how the AI plays against the AI. We have written various tests for the application.

You have learned how Minimax works for turn-based games. You can apply this to other turn-based games as well. If you want to know more on strategies for such games, you can take a look at game theory, the mathematical study of these games.

Reading this means that you have finished the Functional Programming part of this book. One chapter remains, which will explain how you can migrate a legacy JavaScript code base to TypeScript.

10
Migrate JavaScript to TypeScript

In the previous chapters, we have built new applications in TypeScript. However, you might also have old code bases in JavaScript which you want to migrate to TypeScript. We will see how these projects can be converted to TypeScript.

You could rewrite the whole project from scratch, but that would require a lot of work for big projects. Since TypeScript is based on JavaScript, this transition can be done more efficiently.

Since the migration process is dependent on the project, this chapter can only give guidance. For various common topics, this chapter contains a recipe to migrate code. Migrating a project requires knowledge of the frameworks and the structure of the project.

The following steps are related to migrating a code base:

- Gradually migrating to TypeScript
- Adding TypeScript
- Migrating each file
- Refactoring the project

Gradually migrating to TypeScript

As of TypeScript 1.8, it is possible to combine JavaScript and TypeScript in the same project. Thus, you can migrate a project file by file.

During the migration of the files, the project should be working at every step. That way, you can check that the work is going well, and you can still work on the project. If an urgent bug is reported, you do not have to fix it in the old and migrated version; you only have to fix it in the current version.

You can convert the project in the following steps:

- Add the TypeScript compiler to the project
- Migrate each file
- Refactor and enable stricter checks of TypeScript

In the next sections, we will see how these steps can be done.

Adding TypeScript

Before you can convert JavaScript files to TypeScript, you must add the TypeScript compiler to a project. If the project already uses a build step, the TypeScript compiler must be integrated into the build step. Otherwise, a new build step must be created. In the following sections, we will set up TypeScript and the build system.

Configuring TypeScript

In all cases, you should start with configuring TypeScript. This configuration will be used by code editors and the build tool. The most important setting is `allowJs`. This setting allows JavaScript files in the TypeScript project. Other important options are target and module. For target, you can choose between `es3`, `es5`, and `es2015`. The latest version of JavaScript, `es2015`, is not supported in all browsers at the time of writing. You can target `es2015` when you write an application for NodeJS. You can target `es5` for browsers. For very old environments, you must target `es3`.

If the project uses external modules, you should also set the `module` setting. If your project uses **CommonJS**, mostly used in combination with NodeJS, browserify or webpack, you should use `"module"`: `"commonjs"`. An import in CommonJS can be recognized by a call to require and an export by an assignment to `exports.[...]` or `module.exports`, and files are not wrapped in a `define` function:

```
var path = require("path");

exports.lorem = ...;
module.exports = ...;
```

Another module format is **AMD**, Asynchronous Module Definition. This format is used a lot for web applications. You can configure TypeScript for AMD with `"module"`: `"amd"`. The most popular implementation of AMD is `require.js`.

An AMD file starts with a `define` call.

```
define(["require", "exports", "path"], function (require, exports, path) {
    exports.lorem = ...;
});
```

Recent projects might use `es2015` modules, with a build step. You can recognize such files by the `import` and `export` keywords.

```
import * as path from "path";
export var lorem = ...;
```

If you use `es2015` modules, you can set `"module"`: `"es2015"`. However, since these modules are often used with a certain build step to compile these modules to CommonJS, AMD or SystemJS, you can also do that directly with TypeScript. The TypeScript compiler will also do this transformation for the JavaScript files of the project, so you can remove the other build step that does this (for instance, Babel). If you want to do this, you must use `"commonjs"`, `"amd"`, or `"systemjs"`.

If your project did not use a build step, you might want to change the directory structure of your project. You must not store the source files (TypeScript/JavaScript) in the same directory as the compiled files (JavaScript). In the previous chapters, we used `lib` for the sources and `dist` for the compiled files. We can configure that by setting `"outDir"`: `"dest"`. If you use a build tool such as gulp where temporary files can stay in memory and are not written to the disk, you do not need to set this option since the compiled files are not directly written to the disk.

This should result in a `tsconfig.json` file similar to this one:

```
{
  "compilerOptions": {
    "target": "es5",
    "module": "commonjs",
    "outDir": "dist"
  }
}
```

You should place this file in the directory that contains the source files. If your project did not use a build tool, you can now compile the project with `tsc -p ./lib` (where `./lib` references the directory that contains the source files and `tsconfig.json` file), provided that you have TypeScript installed (`npm install typescript -g`). If your project already used a build system, you have to integrate the TypeScript compiler into it, which we will do in the next section.

Configuring the build tool

Configuring the build depends on the build tool you use. For a few commonly used tools, you can find the steps here. Most build tools require you to install a TypeScript plugin. For browserify, you must install `tsify` using NPM; for Grunt, `grunt-ts`; for gulp, `gulp-typescript`; and for webpack, `ts-loader`. If your project uses JSPM, you do not have to install a plugin.

You can find various configurations with these tools at: `http://www.typescriptlang.or g/docs/handbook/integrating-with-build-tools.html`. If you use a different build tool, you should look in the documentation of the tool and search for a TypeScript plugin.

Since TypeScript accepts (and needs) the JavaScript files in your project, you must provide all source files to the TypeScript compiler. For gulp, that would mean that you add TypeScript before other compilation steps. Imagine a task in your `gulp` file looks like this:

```
gulp.src("lib/**/*.js")
  .pipe(plugin())
  .pipe(gulp.dist("dest"));
```

You can add TypeScript to this `gulp` file:

```
var ts = require("gulp-typescript");
var tsProject = ts.createProject("lib/tsconfig.json");
...
gulp.src("lib/**/*.js")
  .pipe(ts(tsProject))
  .pipe(plugin())
  .pipe(gulp.dist("dest"));
```

For a build tool that cannot store temporary files in memory, such as Grunt, you should compile TypeScript to a temporary directory. Other steps from the build should read the sources from this directory.

For more information on how to configure a specific build tool, you can look at the documentation of the tool and the plugin.

Acquiring type definitions

For dependencies that you use, such as jQuery, you must acquire type definitions. You can install them using `npm`. You can find these type definitions on `https://aka.ms/types`.

Testing the project

Before going to the next step, make sure that the build is working. TypeScript should only show syntax errors in JavaScript files. Also, the application should be working at runtime.

> If you are now using TypeScript to transpile ES modules to CommonJS, you might run into problems. Babel and TypeScript handle default imports differently. Babel looks for the default property, and if that does not exist, it behaves the same as a full module import. TypeScript will only look for the default property. If you get runtime errors after the migration, you might need to replace a default import (`import name from "package"`) with a full module import (`import * as name from "package"`).

Migrating each file

When the build system is set up, you can start with migrating files. It is easiest to start with files that do not depend on other files, as these do not depend on types of other files. To migrate a file, you must rename the file extension to `.ts`, convert the module format to ES modules, correct types that are inferred incorrectly, and add types to `untyped` entities. In the next sections, we will take a look at these tasks.

Converting to ES modules

In TypeScript files you cannot use CommonJS or AMD directly. Instead you must use ES modules, like we did in the previous chapters. For an import, you must choose from these:

- `import * as name from "package"`, imports the whole package, similar to `var name = require("package")` in CommonJS.
- `import name from "package"`, imports the default export, similar to `var name = require("package").default`.
- `import { name } from "package"`, imports a named export, similar to `var name = require("package").name`.

ES modules offer various constructs to export values from modules:

- `export function name() {}`, `export class Name {}`, `export var name`, exports a named variable. Compiles to:

```
function name() {}
exports.name = name;
```

- `export default function name() {}`, `export default class Name {}`, `export default var name`, exports a variable as the default export. Compiles to:

```
function name() {}
exports.default = name;
```

- `export default x`, where x is an expression, exports an expression as the default export.
- `export { x, y }`, exports variables x and y as named exports. This compiles to:

```
exports.x = x;
exports.y = y;
```

With CommonJS and AMD you can also export an expression as the full module, with `module.exports = x` in CommonJS or `return x` in AMD. This is not possible with ES modules. If this pattern is used in a file that you must migrate, you can either switch to an ES export or patch all files that import this file, or use a legacy export statement in TypeScript. With `export = x`, you can export an expression as the full module. However, since this is not standard, it is not advised to do this but it can help during the migration. This compiles to `module.exports = x` or `return x`.

The file should give no syntax errors when you compile it. It might show type errors, which the next session will discuss.

Correcting types

Since the file was a JavaScript file, it does not have any type annotations. At some locations, TypeScript will infer types for variables. When you declare a variable and directly assign to it, TypeScript will infer the type based on the type of the assignment. Thus, when you write `let x = ""`, TypeScript will type x as a `string`. However, in some cases the inferred type is not correct. You can see that in the next examples.

```
let x = {};
x.a = true;
```

The type of x is inferred as `{ }`, an empty object. Thus, the assignment to `x.a` is not allowed, since the property `a` does not exist. You can fix this by adding a type to the definition: `let x: { a?: boolean } = {}`.

```
class Base {
  a: boolean;
}
class Derived extends Base {
  b: string;
}
let x = new Derived();
x = new Base();
```

In this case, the type of x is `Derived`. The assignment on the last line is not allowed, since `Base` is not assignable to `Derived`. You can again fix this by adding a type: `let x: Base = new Derived()`.

If the type of a variable is unknown or very complex, you can use `any` as the type for the variable, which disables type checking for that variable.

Other possible sources of errors are classes. When you use the class keyword to create classes, you can get errors that a property does not exist in the class.

```
class A {
  constructor() {
    this.x = true;
  }
}
```

In this example, you would get an error that the property x does not exist in A. In TypeScript, you must declare all properties of a class.

```
class A {
  x: boolean;
  constructor() {
    this.x = true;
  }
}
```

Most errors of TypeScript should now be fixed. Some cases however can still generate type errors, for example when a variable has different types, which is discussed in the next session.

Adding type guards and casts

A common pattern in JavaScript is that a function accepts either a single value of a certain type, or an array of multiple types. You can express such a type with a union type:

```
function foo(input: string | string[]) {
  ...
}
```

In the body of such a function, you would check if the argument is an array or a single string. In most cases, TypeScript can correctly follow this pattern. For instance, TypeScript can change the type of input in the next example.

```
function foo(input: string | string[]) {
  if (typeof input === "string") {
  } else {

  }
}
```

The type of input is string in the block after the if and string[] in the else-block. The changing of a type is called narrowing and the checks for a type are called **type guards**. TypeScript has built-in support for typeof and instanceof type guards, but you can also define your own. A user defined type guard function is a function that takes the value as one of its arguments and returns true when the value is of a certain type. A type guard can be written like this:

```
function isBar(value: Foo): value is Bar {
  ...
}
```

As you can see, the return type of `isBar` is `value is Bar`, a special `boolean` type. If you have a function that checks that a value is of a certain type, you should add a return type to make it a type guard.

If the TypeScript compiler still cannot correctly narrow the type of a variable on a certain location, you must add a `cast`. A cast is a compiler instruction in which the programmer guarantees that a value is of a certain type. A type guard can be written in two different ways.

```
<Bar> value
value as Bar
```

The first syntax is most used, but not supported in **JSX** or **TSX** files. In a TSX file, you must use the second syntax.

When you have fixed all these errors, the project should compile without errors again.

Using modern syntax

The class keyword was introduced in **ES2015**, a recent version of JavaScript. Older projects created classes with a function and prototypes should migrate to the new class syntax. In TypeScript, these classes can be typed better. Following are two code fragments, which show the same class written with the prototype and with the class syntax.

```
var A = (function () {
    function A() {
        this.x = true;
    }
    A.prototype.a = function () {
    };
    return A;
}());

class A {
  x: boolean;
  constructor() {
    this.x = true;
  }
  a() {
  }
}
```

You can also use the new, block scoped variable declarations. Instead of var x you should write const x for a variable that is not reassigned and let x for a variable that will be reassigned.

Finally, you can also use arrow functions (or lambda expressions). Using normal function definitions, the value of this is lost in callbacks. Thus, you had to store that in a variable (self or _this was commonly used). You can replace that with an arrow function.

```
var _this = this;
function myCallback() {
  _this ...
}
```

This code fragment can be rewritten to:

```
const myCallback = () => {
  this ...
};
```

Adding types

The file compiles now, but lots of variables and parameters might be typed as any. For complex types, you can first create an interface, for object types, or a type alias, for function types or union types.

TypeScript does not infer types in the following cases:

- Variable declaration without an initializer (like var x;)
- Parameters of a function definition without a default value
- Return type of a function that uses recursion

In an editor like VS Code, you can check the type of a variable, parameter or function by hovering over it. On these locations you should add a type annotation yourself.

Refactoring the project

When you have ported the project to TypeScript, you can refactor the program more easily. You should remove patterns that do not fit well with TypeScript. For instance, magic string values should be replaced by enums. When you have a project that uses a framework, you can also do some framework related refactoring. For a React project, you might want to upgrade from the old class creation with React.createClass to the new class syntax.

A proper editor can help during refactoring. VS Code can rename an identifier in the whole project or find all references of an identifier. It can also format your code if it's messy or jump to the definition of an identifier. You can access these options with a right-click on the identifier in the code.

Which steps you must do for refactoring depends on your project. You should look for parts of the code that are not typed or incorrectly typed, because of a bad structure or some dynamic behavior.

Enable strict checks

You can enable stricter checks in TypeScript. These checks can improve the quality of your program. Here are a few options that can be useful.

- `noImplicitAny`: Checks that no variables are typed as any unless you explicitly annotated them with any.
- `noImplicitReturns`: Checks that all execution paths of a function return a value.
- `strictNullChecks`: Enables strict checks for variables that might be undefined or null.

Summary

In this chapter, we have looked at various steps involved in migrating a project from JavaScript to TypeScript. We saw how a project can be migrated gradually. We looked at various ways to update an old project so that it can use new JavaScript features and how it can use the type system of TypeScript. You can use your knowledge from the previous chapters to make the project even better.

Index